AF583290

CHILDCARE CENTER SUCCESS

CHILDCARE

HOW TO MAXIMIZE PROFITS

CENTER

AND MINIMIZE MISTAKES

SUCCESS

GRAFTON MILNE, SIOR, CCIM

FOREWORD BY RON MCGUCKIN

Childcare Center Success: How to Maximize Profits and Minimize Mistakes

For information about this title or to order other books and/or electronic media, contact the publisher:

Grafton Milne
graftonmilne.com
grafton@menlocre.com

ISBNs:
979-8-9854381-0-9 (hardcover with dust jacket)
979-8-9854381-1-6 (eBook)

Printed in the United States of America

Interior design and cover formatting: 1106 Design
Cover design by Speckled Art Co.

Table of Contents

Foreword ix

Preface xiii

Introduction xvii

Section 1: The Basics of the Childcare Industry . . . 1

Do Your Due Diligence 3

Due Diligence 4

How Not to Do It 5

A Good Example of Due Diligence 6

Getting the Most from Professional Advisors . . . 7

A Word of Warning About How This Works 8

Determine Your "How" 9

Be Open to New Information 9

The Most Important Thing About Due Diligence . . . 10

Understand Childcare Regulations and Licensing . . . 11

Hire the Right Experts 15

Don't Cut Corners 18

Find the Right Location 21

Why Location Is Critical 22

Hire the Right Experts to Get Location Right . . . 23

Make a Checklist 25

Section 2: Planning for Success 29
Effective Planning 31
Getting Some Help 32
Business Planning 32
The Planning Sweet Spot. 33
Setting Goals 34
Stress-Testing Your Ideas 37
Creating a Marketing Plan 41
Some Notes About Preparing Your Plan 43
Your Avatar 44
Your Services 45
Your Competition 46
Your Value Proposition 48
Your Marketing Strategy 49
Your Marketing Goals 52
Creating and Using a Budget 53
Some Things You Must Know 55
Bookkeeping Equation 55
You Need a Professional Advisor 57
Creating a Basic Operating Budget 58
Understand the Basics of How Your Business Works 60
Understand How to Keep Up with How You're Doing 60

Section 3: Details of Running Your Center 63
Hiring the Right People 65
What Needs to Be Done 66
The Right People 68
Hiring 70

Onboarding . . . 73
Helping People Grow . . . 75
Management and Operations . . . 77
Your Organization Chart . . . 78
Make Sure Everything Important Gets Done . . . 80
Make Sure Things Get Done Properly . . . 81
Meetings . . . 83
Cost of Care . . . 85
The Big Challenge . . . 86
One More Thing—Be Prepared . . . 88
Your Building . . . 91
Assemble a Building Team . . . 92
Functionality: How Does Your Building Work as a Childcare Center? . . . 93
Design: How Does Your Building Look and Feel? . . . 95
Licensing . . . 97

Conclusion . . . 99
Children Come First . . . 99
Make Your Business as Good as Your Childcare . . . 100
It's All About the "WHO" . . . 101
Always Be Improving . . . 102

Appendices . . . 105
Formal Business Plans for Loan and Grant Applications . . . 107
Cost of Care . . . 115
Reading List . . . 117
Acknowledgments . . . 121
About the Author . . . 125

Foreword

When I first began working in the field of early childhood education more than forty years ago, there were no road maps to success. The field was dominated by Head Start Programs and non-profits that provided "daycare" as a service to the community. These programs were not typically operated for a profit but rather made ends meet through government funding and donations. But there were a few brave women who saw an opportunity to grow a business while pursuing their passion. Generally, these were outstanding early childhood educators without much, if any, business experience.

Much has changed over the last forty years. We have witnessed an explosion of preschools with millions of children enrolled throughout the country. We have even seen childcare take its place as an "essential business" in the American economy. Until now, one thing has remained the same. There have been no concise guides to help those who are drawn to this business.

Author and childcare real estate professional Grafton Milne takes us on a thorough journey into the business of childcare from start to finish in his new book, *Childcare Center Success: How to Maximize Profits and Minimize Mistakes*. He shows us how to perform due diligence, select the right location, deal with the various regulations, assemble a group of experts you can trust, and set your business apart from the others with a good marketing plan. He also shows the importance of hiring and retaining the right people and why it is important for your staff to keep growing. This book is perfect for the outstanding teacher who knows they can run a better center. It is also important for the veteran owner who wants to improve their operation, and the bottom line.

Over the years as I have traveled around the country, I have asked hundreds of owners and directors how much it cost their agency to provide care to one two year old for one day. Almost always I am met with a blank stare and, at best, an inaccurate guess. Grafton shows you how to determine the actual cost of care of each age group or other program component. You will discover where you actually make a profit and where you are investing in the future. Grafton gives you the information you need to make informed decisions about your business.

Most importantly, Grafton Milne reminds us of the importance of remembering that what is good for the children is good for your business. This has been especially true as we make our way through the COVID-19 pandemic. Lagging enrollment, lack of qualified staff, complaining parents, masks, vaccinations, and frequently changing mandates and directives from various government agencies have been some of the difficult challenges childcare centers have faced. Businesses that follow Grafton's advice will be equipped to not only succeed, but to thrive as we face these unexpected challenges. Making decisions with the best interest of children in mind will always lead to success.

Childcare Center Success: How to Maximize Profits and Minimize Mistakes is a must-read for anyone interested in the business of childcare.

—Ronald V. McGuckin, Esq.
President, Association for Early Learning Leaders
Philadelphia, Pennsylvania
September 2021

Preface

A*s we entered the childcare center,* something felt off. I've been in many low-income, low-budget childcare centers in several different markets, but this one was different. A local real estate owner asked me to stop by their shopping center that had a childcare center in it to see what would happen if the current childcare ever vacated.

As I've done many times, I engaged a local licensing consultant to join me to review the property's condition from a licensing standpoint. We were both taken aback by what we found.

The facility looked and smelled like it had never been cleaned. There was food spilled everywhere and dirty dishes piled high. Children were walking around with soiled diapers. My heart ached for these sweet children and their families who probably didn't think they had other options for childcare.

The sweet, little old woman who owned the center got very nervous about showing us one of the classrooms. As she tried to get us to "keep walking," I gently pushed open the door to the classroom, and my heart stopped.

I saw a full bedroom setup with a grown man's wardrobe spread across the floor. I had a sick feeling in the pit of my stomach as I saw a handgun and a lighter with what appeared to be drugs sitting on the counter less than ten feet from a room full of beautiful, innocent little children.

We called the police and waited for them to arrive. We left once we were sure things were properly handled.

That was the moment I knew I could make a difference helping providers understand the importance of having a safe, clean, beautiful childcare center. I know what that kind of center can do for a community and for the owner and staff.

When COVID hit in March of 2020, I felt like I was working triage in an intensive care unit for businesses. The childcare industry faced a tornado of new challenges, restrictions, and regulations. I received countless phone calls from clients, friends, vendors, owners, and directors throughout the industry. They were seeking advice and perspective on how to navigate those interesting times.

We discussed real estate strategies related to the mortgage or lease of their center. We also discussed business and marketing strategies, staffing strategies, and a whole list of other things. After a few weeks of this, I decided it might be time for me to write a book to serve as a resource for others who might be facing similar challenges. This book is the result.

I wanted to communicate to others how successful childcare centers succeed. I reached out to successful operators and childcare experts from around the country.

They graciously shared their experience and knowledge with me. My experience in working with numerous childcare clients at a 30,000-foot-view gives me a unique perspective.

This book is by no means an all-encompassing guide to everything related to the childcare industry. But it is full of principles and wisdom gleaned from many successful childcare centers in many markets from across the country. I hope you'll benefit from my experience and expertise and learn from *Childcare Center Success: How to Maximize Profits and Minimize Mistakes*

—Grafton Milne
Phoenix, Arizona
September 2021

Introduction

"Success leaves clues."
—Jack Canfield, co-author of the *Chicken Soup* books and author of *The Success Principles*

W***hat is a successful childcare center?*** This is one of those questions where you should take the long view. It's easy to think a center is successful when enrollment is high, you've had a good year or two, and you have a "one of a kind" program and business strategy. In my experience, truly successful centers have two things in common.

A way of elevating and inspiring everyone around them. The children they've cared for use what they've learned in childcare throughout their educations and throughout their lives. Truly successful childcare centers enrich families, and communities as well. You'll discover how successful centers do it in the pages ahead.

Truly successful childcare centers are well run. They comply with the array of licensing regulations with little pushback. Taxes are paid on time. The center is well maintained. Truly successful childcare centers make enough profit to pay the owners and teachers a sustainable income. They have a sufficient business acumen so the center can deliver quality childcare year after year. It's not easy, but you'll learn how successful centers do it.

Is This Book for You?

I wrote this book for people who are passionate about childcare and who want to own a childcare center. Some are new to the industry. Take Ted Batycki and his wife, Genna.

They own Natural Choice Academy in Phoenix. Before they opened their center in 2011, Ted was an experienced commercial banker. Ted says that they "absolutely went into owning our childcare business because we wanted something for our own children."

Ted had a full toolbox of analytical tools from his education, and experience as a banker. His challenge was to learn to use those skills in a childcare center. If you're like Ted, coming from business to childcare, that will be your challenge. I'll show you how tools like budgeting and facilities management can be used successfully. You'll also learn about some of the regulatory and operational requirements that are unique to childcare.

I also wrote this book for people who were experienced in the childcare industry but maybe have never run a childcare center before. Barbie Prinster is now the program manager at the Arizona Early Childhood Education Association. She describes an experience early in her career, when she became an assistant director in a childcare center, this way:

> *When I took over as an assistant director, I knew childcare. I could go into any classroom and make it work. But now, I'm in charge of a business. And now, I have labor percentages to work with. And now, I have a budget, and I have all these different line items. And I had to learn how to do all of that.*

If you're in a situation like Barbie's, where you know the childcare part but not the business part, I wrote this book for you.

Simple Truths

If you're looking for riches or easy money, you need to try another field. Barbie Prinster says she sees too many people who think that childcare is easy, "like babysitting." You can make a decent living from childcare. The psychological rewards can be great. But if you're thinking about making millions, your odds are probably better if you buy a lottery ticket.

Childcare is about caring for and educating children. If you believe that, you will probably gravitate toward the childcare tasks of your center. It's important to do that well.

But if you don't pay attention to fundamental business practices, you'll have a hard time and may wind up without a center to run. You won't be able to have a truly successful center unless you take care of the business.

You must manage the accounting so that taxes and fees are paid on time. You must deal with licensing issues and facilities management. You must learn to hire and supervise well. You must hire excellent teachers and pay them competitively. You must master the basics of marketing, otherwise, your center won't be around for very long.

Four Important Concepts

I packed a lot of information and knowledge into this book. You'll find many topics, ideas, and suggestions, but there are four important concepts that run through the book. You'll come upon them again and again.

Children come first. This is "childcare," and children are the most important part of it. They're why we do it. Ted Batycki said this much more eloquently than I could. Here are his words:

> *What's right for children is right for our business. We ask ourselves that question all the time. And so, we talk about our business. We understand the finances, we understand how to make money in this business. But we always ask ourselves, "Are we doing this because it's right for the children or are we doing it because it's right for the business?" And if it's only because it's right for the business, that's not a good reason to do it.*

Don't try to do it alone. No matter how smart you are, no matter how experienced you are, you can't master everything you need to know to run a truly successful childcare center. It's not likely that you're a CPA, and even if you are, you probably don't know much about constructing and building out a childcare center. That's why you need experts. Experts can help you with specialized situations and systems. Besides experts, you can go to other childcare operators for help and advice. This truly is a case where all of us are smarter than any one of us.

Develop the habits of success. True childcare success is built on the hundreds of actions throughout each day. Use tools that can help you be more effective, such as checklists and reminders. Set things up so that regular things are done routinely. The small tasks you do right every day are the foundation of true childcare success.

Elana Hillel is the co-owner of the Premier Learning Academy and an experienced childcare entrepreneur. She recommends habits that keep you from having to solve every problem from scratch.

Elana suggests using a giant wall calendar so everyone can see what's going on for the month. Set alarms on your smartphone to remind you of things to do during the day.

Develop the habit of staying in touch with peers to share ideas and insights and help each other solve problems. One common name for a group like this is a "mastermind group." The idea originated with Napoleon Hill who described it in his book, *Think and Grow Rich*. Thanks to modern communication technology you can create a mastermind group with peers who live anywhere.

One of the most important "habits of success" is working with a "growth mindset." The term comes from Carol

Dweck's excellent book, *Mindset: The New Psychology of Success*. In the book, Dweck describes mindset this way:

> *Mindset change is not about picking up a few pointers here and there. It's about seeing things in a new way. When people... change to a growth mindset, they change from a judge-and-be-judged framework to a learn-and-help-learn framework. Their commitment is to growth, and growth take plenty of time, effort, and mutual support.*

Success leaves clues. Learn from successful childcare center operators. Be on the lookout for new practices that work. Attend meetings and conferences. Read books and articles for ideas about what you can do better. Form a network of alliances in your area to share ideas.

What's in This Book?

I divided this book into three sections. The Basics of the Childcare Industry, Planning for Success, and Details of Running Your Center.

There are three chapters in "The Basics of the Childcare Industry" section. The first is "Do Your Due Diligence." You'll discover examples of good and bad due diligence processes, and you'll learn that the most important thing about due diligence is doing it. In the second chapter, "Understand Childcare Regulations and Licensing," I emphasize choosing the right experts for each aspect of compliance. And you'll get the critical advice not to cut corners. The final chapter is called “Find the Right Location.” Here, I explain why finding a good location is critical to your success and why you should hire experts who will help you identify a good location and negotiate a successful purchase or rental agreement.

The second section in the book is called “Planning for Success.” I wanted to make this something that would be simple and effective, whether you have business experience or not. The first chapter in this section is titled “Effective Planning.” You’ll learn about setting goals and what I call “the planning sweet spot.” The next two chapters, “Creating a Marketing Plan” and “Creating and Using a Budget,” outline simple plans that will help you achieve success and keep track of how you’re doing. You’ll learn not only how to create an effective marketing plan and an effective budget, but also how to use them optimally.

The final section of the book is about the details of running your center. The first chapter is about hiring the right people. If you hire the right people, support them, and treat them fairly, success is almost assured. Several of the people I interviewed thought hiring and supervising was the hardest part of running a childcare center.

The second chapter in this section is about management and operations. You’ll learn how to make sure all the important things get done properly. You’ll also learn about an important center management concept called “cost of care.” The final chapter is about your building. You’ll learn how to make sure your building will help you provide effective and profitable childcare. You’ll also learn about the importance of maintenance to help you stay in compliance with childcare regulations.

So, let's get after it. Let's dive right in and start with the basics of the childcare industry.

SECTION 1

The Basics of the Childcare Industry

The childcare industry is unique. Federal, state, and local regulations determine a lot of what you can and can't do. Understanding the basics of the childcare industry is the first step to running a successful center.

In the first chapter of this section, "Do Your Due Diligence," you'll learn the basics of due diligence. Due Diligence is doing your homework, so you can make wise decisions about how to proceed. You should conduct due diligence before making any important decision. The chapter discusses due diligence if you're considering opening a childcare center.

You'll also learn how to get the most from professional advisors. You can't know or find out everything you need to know by yourself. It's easy to get caught up in the emotion of the moment. Knowledgeable and dispassionate professional advice is critical to making sound business decisions.

Doing due diligence on any important decision is a success habit. It's important in childcare to do right by the children and comply with childcare regulations and licensing requirements.

The next chapter, "Understand Childcare Regulations and Licensing," explains that federal, state, and local government all regulate childcare. The regulations were put there to keep the children safe. Your challenge is to be aware of and comply with all those regulations.

Hiring the right experts to help you is crucial. It's especially important when you're making a big decision, like where to locate or how to design your center.

"Finding the Right Location," the third and final chapter of this section, concerns one of the most important decisions you will make. You must buy or lease a location that helps you meet all government requirements. It must also be exactly right for your unique center.

The right location will let you create effective and safe learning environments for your children. The right location is convenient for client families. The right location will also be priced so you can be profitable enough to provide quality care for a long time. Having the right advisors will help improve your odds of making wise business decisions.

Do Your Due Diligence

T***homas Edison may have been*** the most prolific inventor in history. Among his more than one thousand U.S. patents are ones for the phonograph, motion pictures, and the incandescent lightbulb. Since I was little, I've heard stories about how it took Edison thousands of tries to get the lightbulb right.

By the time Edison was working on the lightbulb, he had created an "invention factory" in Menlo Park, New Jersey. Edison staffed it with people with all kinds of talents and set them to work making inventions.

Edison had income from many earlier inventions. He had staff, equipment, and resources. The muckers were turning out other inventions that would generate income. He could afford to try one thousand things before he found the one that worked. Most of us don't have that luxury. If you want to open and operate a successful childcare center, you can't try a thousand options to find one that works.

There's a lot on your plate. You must decide what kind of center you'll have and whether you'll be private pay or subsidized. You must decide the kind of curriculum you're going to offer and what hours you'll be open. There are licensing requirements, zoning requirements, and state, federal, and local regulations you must follow. Whatever kind of childcare center you plan to open, you must find good people to work for you and you must work out the finances so you can stay afloat.

Due Diligence

Due diligence is the process of researching and analyzing everything you must consider so your childcare venture can be a success. There are formal definitions of due diligence, such as the one on the Investopedia website: "Due diligence is an investigation, audit, or review performed to confirm the facts of a matter under consideration."

That's fancy wording, but the meaning is simple. Due diligence is doing your homework so you know what you're getting yourself into: the good, the bad, and the ugly. It's making sure you know everything you have to do so you can plan for it. It's heading off nasty surprises.

As I mentioned earlier, Elana Hillel and her sister, Leora, are co-owners of the Premier Learning Academy in Chandler, Arizona. Here's how she describes due diligence when it comes to buying a center:

> *Always getting someone to audit the place for you before you buy it and looking into their ProCare [childcare management software] and CRM [customer relationship management software]. I really like to*

see how many people are on your email database. It's very, very important. And the next best thing is your market research. I think that first, you've got to have the money, and then you've got to know who to spend it on.

I'll cover many of the things you need to think about and prepare for in this book. I'll point you to other sources of information, too. But before we move on, let me share stories of two different people who wanted to open a childcare center and took vastly different approaches to their due diligence.

How Not to Do It

A woman came to me and asked me to find a location for her new childcare center. She had received a few pieces of real estate in a family trust when a family member passed away. She liquidated all the assets and moved to Phoenix. Since she had some experience in childcare, she ended up getting connected with a childcare franchisee and bought the rights to a franchise location in Phoenix. There was no way she could fail, she thought, since she had so much money.

I introduced her to a developer and investor I've done a lot of business with, and he acquired a piece of real estate for her. We helped her sign a very favorable lease that included several months' of free rent. We also negotiated a favorable tenant improvement allowance for her that would make the building beautiful. It was going to be a nice, new, beautiful childcare center in a great area.

I tried to guide her through who she needed to talk with and what the right processes would be. But she just said, "Oh, no, I'll figure it out. My friend knows who I need to talk to." She wouldn't let me coach her through the process.

Before we knew it and before she hired a single employee, she had burned through all the free rent. Eventually, she defaulted on the lease and wound up being sued. At that point, she should have been in business, but she didn't even have a childcare license. Even if parents were knocking on the door trying to come to her, she couldn't enroll their children.

Let's analyze why she failed. She believed that she would succeed because she had a lot of money. Money's important, but it never guarantees success. The woman didn't know what she didn't know. That's common, but she wasn't willing to learn from people who did know. Finally, she didn't act on what she knew but rather let the grass grow under her feet. In other words, she did just about everything wrong. Let's look now at an example of someone who did everything right.

A Good Example of Due Diligence

I recently met with a client who was looking to expand her childcare business into another part of town. We worked through my strategic processes and procedures to ensure that she had all her ducks in a row. It was easy because she had done so much work before she contacted me.

She had a beautiful, well-thought-out business plan and a marketing plan. She had a poster-board-size map of her target community on which she marked the locations of all her potential competitors. She also indicated the locations of the schools and largest businesses in the area. She had information on demographic reports and traffic counts.

She was a childcare expert, and she did her homework. My job was to guide her through the real estate decision, which I was happy to do. She made it easy for me to help her succeed.

This woman did it right. She knew that she would have to work to succeed. She knew the business, and she talked to experts to learn more. Because she did so much due diligence, it was easy for professional advisors to help her.

Getting the Most from Professional Advisors

It's important to figure out how you'll make your center successful. But you can't do it alone. You can't possibly know everything important about childcare laws, finances, licensing requirements, the community, and operating your center. That's why you need professional advisors.

Part of doing due diligence is knowing who to talk to. You'll almost always need an attorney to mitigate your risk, an accountant to assist in underwriting, and a commercial real estate agent who knows childcare and can help you find a building that meets all of your requirements. We'll discuss this in more detail later in the book.

Every situation and every professional is unique, but most of us follow essentially the same process with a new client. I'll illustrate by describing how I work when a person contacts me.

Usually, they've either been referred to me by a specific person, or they've heard my name from colleagues or friends in the industry and they contact me via phone or email, and we set up an appointment.

I want to be a resource for them and set them up for success. We all win that way. My first step is to learn about them and their experience, especially in childcare. And I want to know their goals, what they are looking to do. I want to learn as much as possible so I can be as helpful as possible.

I also want to determine if they have some business acumen. Many people who start a childcare center are knowledgeable and passionate when it comes to childcare. But they often have little to no business experience. Do they have a marketing plan or a business plan? I want to hear how they intend to finance their center.

I want to know if they've done a competitive analysis. They need to differentiate their center from all the other childcares in their area. Are they going to be more of a private pay, specialized curriculum-based program, or use a more state-funded, bring-them-all, take-them-all approach?

A Word of Warning About How This Works

When we put the parts of due diligence into a list, it's easy to think that you should tackle them one right after the other. It doesn't work that way in real life.

You'll find that working on one area sparks ideas for another area. For instance, you may work on your business plan and realize you must decide how many people you should hire. When you work on management and staff, you may also need to think about regulations and licensing.

Work through your due diligence with your professional advisors until you're sure you've done as much as you can.

Determine Your "How"

Due diligence is about learning what you need to know so you can make your center successful. That's important. It's also important to think about another "how."

How will you make a difference in the community? How do you plan to be a positive influence in the lives of the families that choose your center over other centers?

Don't just think about the dollars and cents and location and regulations. Spend time thinking about how what you do will affect the families you serve and the community at large.

Be Open to New Information

The due diligence process is not just a way to determine whether or not to proceed. Sometimes you will uncover new information that offers you the opportunity to change your original plan.

I once helped an owner with her due diligence process for a planned move into a new area. During the process, she learned that the area had more stay-at-home moms than she originally thought. She adjusted her plan to account for the new information. When I played quarterback, we called that "calling an audible."

The Most Important Thing About Due Diligence

The most important aspect of due diligence is to just do it!

Effective due diligence increases your odds of success. You can plan some things. You can anticipate some issues. There will be things you can only think about after you're up and running.

Use this book as a guide to doing your due diligence. For most childcare operators, due diligence starts with learning about childcare regulations and licensing requirements, which we will cover in detail in our next chapter.

Understand Childcare Regulations and Licensing

There's no magic in magic, it's all in the details.
—Walt Disney

Childcare ***regulations*** and licensing requirements are there to keep children safe. They can be very intimidating if this is your first childcare center. Don't worry, thousands of people before you have navigated these regulations. To do it successfully, you need help, and you need to do your due diligence.

The great architect Ludwig Mies van der Rohe could have been talking about meeting childcare regulations and licensing requirements when he said the words quoted above. Here's just one example.

To get a childcare license, you must have an architect stamp your floor plan. He or she will make sure that everything meets proper code. The plumbing must be in the right place. The sanitation stations, access to fire exits, and everything else must meet licensing requirements.

Regulations can cover seemingly small things. You might think that the location of a changing station doesn't matter. But you must be able to visually observe the children in your care while you're changing a diaper. You can't do that if the changing station is facing away from the room.

Start your due diligence by learning which regulations you must comply with and which licensing requirements you must meet. Here are three good places to start:

The U.S. Department of Health and Human Services has created a national database of childcare regulations. It's a tool for finding and searching state licensing requirements. The database includes government agency contact information. Here's the URL:

https://childcareta.acf.hhs.gov/licensing

Another great resource is the Ronald V. McGuckin and Associates website. Ron is a nationally-known expert on childcare provider law. That's even the name of his website: ChildProviderLaw. The link below is to the document center. You'll find many informative documents that will help you do a better job as a provider.

http://www.childproviderlaw.com/index.php
/document-center/

Another information-rich website is run by Child Care Aware® of America. Their site includes a list of resources by state.

https://www.childcareaware.org/our-issues/research/

No matter how many great websites you find or how much you read, there are too many regulations and requirements by too many governmental agencies for you to understand them all and keep up with changes. That's why you should find a local professional to help with your licensing. He or she should be familiar with national, state, and local child-care regulations.

There are several things to be mindful of throughout the process. The first item is one I'm familiar with as a real estate professional.

Zoning requirements vary depending on the city or town where you want to locate. If a property has not been properly zoned, the process can drastically delay your plans for opening or even prevent you from opening at all. A real estate professional with expertise in childcare will help guide you through the process. They will ensure you do not lease or purchase a property prematurely.

I also asked several other professionals to share their experiences on other licensing issues they've run into. Here are some examples that they shared with me.

Robert Haggard of Fleming West Building Company talked about the Americans with Disabilities Act (ADA). You must make sure your facility meets all ADA requirements. This also applies to the playground area. Your childcare expert developer or contractor can assist in any of the zoning, licensing, fire, health, building code inspections, and approvals.

Keith Slater from Slater Insurance who specializes in childcare insurance told me about insurance coverage. Like most small businesses, childcare centers must have insurance in place. In addition to general liability insurance, childcare centers may need to provide medical benefits to staff, workers compensation, and so on. Find an insurance agency that specializes in childcare and ask them to see which policies and plans are best suited for you and your center.

Childcare licensing consultant Raegina Rico shared three areas to be aware of.

You will probably need a certificate of occupancy for your center. Your local planning and development department can provide you information on what's required for a childcare center in your area.

Your local fire department can provide you a list of any safety regulations and requirements you'll need. You might want to point out required locations for doors and how they should open, an evacuation plan, and fire extinguishers. A local architect or contractor who has expertise in childcare can assist here.

Your center must follow Health Department guidelines. Regulations may include cleanliness, kitchen and food preparation, sanitation stations, and pest control.

This is not a comprehensive list, by any means. I included it to give you an idea of the kinds of things you should be aware of. It won't always be easy, but you must approach things with the attitude that you and the licensing surveyor are on the same team. Lori Buxton, Managing Director for the Association for Early Learning Leaders, puts that very well.

> *You have to settle in yourself that licensing is your partner. It may at times be a difficult partner, but you're on the same team, that you understand that their heartbeat is actually the same as yours, and that is to provide a safe, healthy environment for young children to be cared for and educated. Even when you get pushback, and you will, even when you get a no when you want a yes, even when your personality doesn't mesh with the other person's personality, that you show up with the heart and the intent to work together as a team to get where we all want to go.*

A partnership attitude and a willingness to learn will get you a long way. But you must supplement that by hiring the right experts to advise you.

Hire the Right Experts

I don't give advice in areas where I'm not an expert. There's too much at stake. But because I've done a lot of work in childcare and know a lot of people, I often get calls about licensing and the childcare business in general. When that happens, I try to connect childcare owners with local experts I know who seem to fit their needs. At that point, I'm part of a network like the one you need to locate to find out who the best local experts are in your area.

"Local" is a key word here. Many of the regulations and licensing requirements are national in scope, but childcare is a local business. Choose experts who can help you apply national, state, and local regulations to your unique situation.

You probably already have an accountant. That's a good place to start. If your accountant has worked with other childcare centers, he or she will have a good idea of who the experts are and can refer you.

You probably already have friends in the industry. Get their recommendations about the best experts to contact. They should also know enough about you to know what kind of experts fit your personal style and situation.

Work your network. Tell your friends, colleagues, and loved ones that you're starting a childcare business. Work your network to find the best experts to help you with the licensing of your childcare center. The stakes are too high to get this part wrong.

Here's one example from my experience. A woman contacted me after she had spent several months and $100,000 in legal fees purchasing a property. Despite her efforts, she lamented, "now the city is saying they will not allow a childcare center at the location I chose." She hired a different attorney who was a land use attorney who had experience in childcare issues. He referred the woman to me for expert help with real estate issues.

We quickly reassessed market options. With the right attorney, contractor, and architect, we were able to find her childcare company a beautiful property that was a huge upgrade from the property she had spent all that time and money on.

That experience reminds me of a story in one of my favorite books, *Think and Grow Rich* by Napoleon Hill. It's about the experience of a fellow named R. U. Darby.

Darby's uncle caught "gold fever" and headed West to find his fortune. He stopped in Colorado, staked his claim, and set to work with a pick and shovel. Amazingly, he found a huge vein of gold. He needed some special machinery to extract the gold.

He quietly covered up the mine and went home to Maryland. There, he convinced some friends and relatives to put up the money for the machinery. He convinced Darby to go back to Colorado with him to mine the gold.

Tests indicated that the gold was among the finest anyone had found. The uncle and Darby started mining it themselves. Soon, they could pay off their debts, and shortly after that, they would make a killing and never work again.

For a while, things went well, but then they couldn't find any more gold. They knew it was there, so they kept digging. Weeks went by. No luck. Finally, Darby and his uncle gave up. They sold the mining equipment to a junk dealer and went back home.

The junk dealer hired a mining engineer to evaluate the claim. The engineer discovered that Darby and his uncle failed because they weren't familiar with fault lines. The rich vein of gold they sought was there alright. In fact, it was just three feet from where they stopped digging.

The junk man got rich. He didn't know any more than Darby and his uncle about gold mining. He didn't know a thing about fault lines. But he got expert advice and heeded it. He didn't try to go it alone or do things on the cheap. Moral of the story: hire the right experts.

Don't Cut Corners

You will be tempted to do some things yourself because it will save money. In our DIY ("do it yourself") digital age, don't be tempted. This isn't something you can find on Pinterest. Unless you're already an expert or working with expert advice, don't do it. You've got to be patient enough to do it the right way. If you don't, you could be in a world of hurt. You could be delayed 90, 120, or 150 days from opening just because of licensing.

One childcare provider decided that they could install the fire exit signs themselves and save a few bucks. After all, how hard could it be? Well, they put in the fire exit signs but put them in the wrong places. This triggered the licensing surveyor to take extra care with the rest of the inspection. As a result, their opening was delayed 90 days.

Another provider installed the doors in their center to save on labor expense. The problem was they installed doors that opened inward, into the hallway, rather than into the classroom. Their opening was delayed several weeks.

When it comes to complying with licensing requirements, don't seize the opportunity to show off your DIY skills. You could have huge problems just because you tried to save a few bucks. Rob Haggard puts it this way:

> *I would really advise against doing anything yourself when it comes to a project like this and spend the time and take the advice of others and put together a solid team to make it a successful project.*

Do your due diligence. Find out as much as you can about the licensing requirements you must meet. Search out the best local experts you can. Then, listen to them. Resist the urge to do things on your own just to save a little money.

Childcare licensing regulations say a lot about the kind of physical facility you can have and where you can locate it. That's what we're going to cover in the next chapter.

Find the Right Location

"The three most important things in real estate are location, location, and location."

I ***'m sure you've heard that saying.*** More often than not this is a true statement as it relates to commercial real estate, however it might not always be true for your child care center.

In commercial real estate, you want a location that will help you attract customers and do more business. Retail businesses typically want to be located "at the corner." Like a retail store, you want a location where your clients can find you. You also want to be where it's convenient for them to drop off their children and pick them up. You also want a building where you can deliver your services efficiently.

I recently helped a client through the site selection process to determine "the perfect spot" for her next center. We dug deep into demographics, growth and development trends, and traffic counts in the area. We considered the cost for land, the cost to build, and the size of the facility needed.

We made sure the location we chose would enable the center to meet all the national, state, and local regulations and zoning requirements. The facility made it possible for her to serve her customers well and do so at a profit.

When we were through, we had a location that checked all her boxes. I loved hearing praise from various vendors about what an amazing location we found for a childcare center.

In this chapter, you'll learn why location is so important for your childcare center. You'll learn why hiring the right experts is important and how to do it. And you'll learn to create a checklist that makes sure you don't miss anything important along the way. Let's start with the why behind the how.

Why Location Is Critical

Getting the right location is critical to the success of your childcare center. But there's a catch. There's no one kind of location that's perfect for every childcare center. The key is finding the right location for *your* center.

Not everyone needs to be or wants to be on the hard corner of Main and Main. Some people might have a specialized curriculum such as a Mandarin/Spanish immersion Montessori school. That's much more of a destination location. This type of center needs to be closer to a freeway or in an area with a certain demographic makeup.

Location, location, location means different things to different childcare programs. I want to emphasize that you need to understand your business and your clientele to know what the right location is for you.

Location is also critical because decisions about where to locate and what kind of facility you choose have long-term implications. Ted Batycki of Natural Choice Academy in Phoenix, Arizona, sums it up well.

> *The mistakes that you can make in real estate will last a very, very long time. And so, it is absolutely worth spending a tremendous amount of energy thinking about a real estate strategy and working with people who can help execute that strategy.*

Finding the right location is critical. That's why it's critical that you hire the right experts.

Hire the Right Experts to Get the Location Right

The right expert to help you acquire or rent a childcare center is a commercial broker. (In the commercial industry we refer to agents or realtors as Brokers.) That's because commercial real estate transactions are vastly different from buying or renting a home, townhome, condo, or apartment. The commercial process is dramatically different than the residential process. This is where a reputable commercial real estate agent is critical to your success. Here are some things to look for.

Professionalism. There are two designations that signal a broker is in the upper echelon of commercial real estate brokers in the industry. CCIM stands for Certified Commercial

Investment Member. Another global designation in the commercial real estate industry is SIOR, which stands for Society of Industrial and Office Realtors. The SIOR website says we are "the most knowledgeable, experienced, and successful commercial real estate brokerage specialists" in the world. In addition, you need a professional who understands the many credentials or designations of the childcare industry. There's no special designation for brokers who specialize in childcare, but either of those designations indicate outstanding professionalism, expertise, and experience.

Childcare experience. Childcare facilities must meet a range of zoning and licensing requirements. You want a broker who has the experience to prove they can serve childcare clients. Ask for and contact references.

A network of experts. When you meet with a commercial broker, ask about their network of expertise. A broker experienced in childcare should be able to refer to attorneys, architects, and contractors who are also experienced with childcare centers.

Comfort and communication. Your broker should answer your questions in a way that you understand. Your broker should also return calls, texts, and emails promptly. Good communication is critical to any successful relationship.

The right expert will help you navigate the nuances of the childcare industry. Your facility will have to comply with federal, state, and local standards. Decisions about room size and configuration can affect the number of children you have in your center, and thus affect your profitability as we'll discuss later in Section 3 in the chapter on

Management and Operations where we talk about the Cost of Care Analysis.

Choosing the right experts is important, but there's one more thing. You want to get the most out of your experts as possible. A tool that will help you is a checklist.

Make a Checklist

Airline pilots have thousands of hours of experience, but they use checklists on every flight. They use checklists because there's a lot to remember, and missing something could be catastrophic. That's the same reason you should use a checklist when you're looking for a location for your childcare center.

Preparing a checklist forces you to think through the details of your childcare operations and how they determine the kind of facility you need.

A checklist improves communication between you and your experts and between the experts themselves. This ensures everyone is on the same page.

The palest ink is stronger than the strongest memory. When you use your checklist, you don't have to depend on your memory to make sure you check everything. There are several great note taking and or checklist generating apps on most mobile devices.

Your brain has limited capacity. In many cases, you are currently running or operating an existing childcare center. You don't have the mental and emotional bandwidth to remember everything. When you use a checklist, you free up brainpower that you can use for creative decision-making.

Before you start putting your checklist together, write out a description of your ideal client. Some people call that an "avatar." Where do they live? What do they need? What kind of facilities must you have to give them what they need? Starting with a description of your ideal customer, what they need, and how you can meet their needs will help you identify the important facility requirements. We'll discuss the idea of creating an avatar in Section 2 in the chapter on Creating a Marketing Plan.

When you meet with your experts, share the description of your ideal customer. Before you consider any location, read over your description so it's fresh in your mind.

Start creating your checklist by looking at checklists that already exist. Here are some items you can start with.

- Location (submarket) to target
- Size needs for the space (consider your cost of care analysis)
- Signage and visibility
- Proper zoning
- Lot size
- Accessibility to the site (like proximity to freeway, shopping), etc.
- Parking requirements (pick up/drop off)
- Tenant improvement needs
- Exclusivity

This is just a start. Take the time to look at some other lists and add to or modify your own. Kaplan's Location

Guidelines and Worksheets are an excellent resource. Ron Duhart from Kaplan suggests you take an active approach to this process.

> *Make sure you're following the guidelines. Ask questions. Communicate with other childcare centers. Ask them what they experienced when they opened.*

Don't do this all in one go. Put your list together over a few days or a week. This is not something you want to rush.

Taking time to create your checklist makes good use of your brain. Your brain will work on the problem while you're doing other things. You'll find ideas and questions popping into your head. Be prepared to capture them or you'll forget them. Have paper and pen or have a running note on your phone. Most smartphones these days have that capability . . . or, if you're like me, have a waterproof notepad in your shower.

Finding the right location for your childcare center can set you up for success. Remember, there is a good location for your center, but every childcare center's situation is unique. You must find the right place for you.

Choose qualified experts to help you find a location. This is no time to go it alone. Use a checklist to make sure you don't miss anything important. My company developed a proprietary tool we call the "Ideal Space Needs Assessment." It's available on our company's website.

In this section, we've reviewed the basics of the childcare industry. You learned why due diligence is important and the basics of what to investigate. We covered childcare regulations and licensing briefly, stressing the importance of working with knowledgeable experts. Finally, this chapter covered finding the right location for your center.

In the next section, you'll learn about planning for success for your center. We'll cover the basics of effective planning and introduce you to two simple plans that will guide your operations.

SECTION 2

Planning for Success

Planning can be an intimidating subject. Search Amazon for "planning" and you'll find countless resources. Some "simplified" guides run more than two hundred pages. They may make interesting and helpful reading for someone whose job is planning for a large business, but you don't need that level of detail. I've tried to make this section understandable and helpful whether you have business experience or not.

There are three chapters in this section. The first chapter is "Effective Planning." Some centers don't plan much or at all. They barely survive from crisis to crisis. Other centers plan several years in excruciating detail. They're spending time and attention on planning they could use to make their center more successful. You'll learn about how to find the planning sweet spot, between the extremes. You'll discover the latest tools for setting goals and stress-testing them.

The other two chapters in this section demonstrate how to apply the basic principles covered in "Effective Planning." They go into detail about two simple plans that successful childcare centers use.

The next chapter, “Creating a Marketing Plan,” starts by describing what I call a “Home Alone” marketing plan. Marketing is important because it’s the way you keep your classrooms and waiting list full. I cover everything you need to create a simple and effective marketing plan.

The third chapter is called “Creating and Using a Budget.” That may surprise you if you’ve never thought of a budget as a plan. But a budget is a simplified financial plan that you will use frequently to figure out how you’re doing and identify problems early. Budgeting is also a topic that many of the people I interviewed said they had to learn when they established their own center.

Effective Planning

"If you fail to plan, you are planning to fail."
—Attributed to Benjamin Franklin

That's good advice, whether Benjamin Franklin said it or not. Since you bought this book, you probably don't need to be told that planning is important. You know your challenge is to create a great plan.

Early in my career, I worked for a company that sold business and marketing plan outlines for small businesses. According to the Bureau of Labor Statistics, 20 percent of all small businesses fail in their first two years. Almost half are gone by year five.

Investopedia says the top two reasons businesses fail are lack of market research and poor or no planning. I noticed that the businesses we sold our plans to and who implemented those plans were much more likely to not only survive but thrive.

Starting and managing a small business, including a childcare center, is a unique challenge. One book that will help you understand what it's like is *The E-Myth* by Michael

Gerber. The book uses the example of Sally and her pie shop to demonstrate why many people who start a small business fail. Sally knows how to make pies. But she doesn't understand how to run a profitable business.

You may be in the same situation. You may be passionate about caring for children. You might have been a teacher for five, ten, or twenty-plus years. You may know a lot about childcare. But you must master the skills of running a profitable business in order to have a successful childcare center.

Getting Some Help

Top athletes and performers of all kinds use a coach to help them keep improving. Successful businesspeople also use coaches. I've used a few business coaches to help me identify opportunities, avoid costly mistakes, and stay on track with my plans. I strongly recommend that you get regular coaching to help you do the same.

I currently use an organization called Strategic Coach. They've helped me learn to be more productive. They've helped me learn about things I needed to do but of which I had no experience. There's a lot of great tools and resources on time management, creating and managing a great team, creating systems and processes for your business, thinking bigger, and much more. It's ideal for anyone looking to maximize their small business, including childcare.

Business Planning

There are two kinds of business plans. You may need a formal business plan to obtain funding. In the Appendices to this book, you'll learn how to prepare one of those if you need to. Right now, let's discuss simpler plans that you can use to guide your operations and track how you're doing.

The Planning Sweet Spot

There are books filled with instructions on how to plan. With all that advice and wisdom at the click of a mouse, you'd think that every business, including every childcare center, would plan effectively. They don't. I've seen three ways childcare centers fail at planning.

Some don't plan or don't plan enough. They're constantly surprised by things that are likely to happen. A simple one I see all the time is failing to plan for when your rent payments will increase. The majority of the lease transactions I've been involved in have some form of rental escalation built into the rent. If you don't plan for that increase, your budget gets thrown off.

Other centers try to plan every detail years and years out. That sounds good in theory but it doesn't work in practice. A better idea is to plan just enough that you can still be flexible and adjust to changing circumstances.

I've seen other centers that plan and plan and plan but never get to the actual doing. It's like a sports team that practices constantly but never plays a game. I think people do that because planning is a controllable environment. When you plan, you can adjust things so everything comes out well. In real life, that just doesn't happen.

Right now you may be thinking, "Hey, I don't want to do all this planning and budgeting and stuff. I got into childcare because I love children." You don't have to love it, or even like it, but you must do it so you can have a successful center and do the things you love. Lori Buxton put it this way:

> *For me, doing the work with the finances and the strategic planning is what I have to do to get to my reward, which is the people.*

There are no perfect plans, so don't waste time trying to come up with one. Earlier in life, what seems like ages ago, when I played quarterback, I would step up to the line with a plan or play in mind. But sometimes the defense was in a different coverage than what I anticipated. I had to adjust. I had audibles that I could use to call something different.

Just enough planning means planning and action together. Plan enough that you're not surprised but not so much that you don't act. Then, move forward, learning as you go. Begin by setting goals. You'd be surprised at how much you can learn about yourself and your business by doing.

Setting Goals

Gary Latham and Edwin Locke have been researching goals and goalsetting for decades. In 2002, they published an article in *American Psychologist* that identified three ways that goals can help you perform better. Setting goals forces you to make choices. Setting goals gives you energy. And setting goals makes you more persistent.

There are three different timeframes for setting goals. The furthest out is what Jim Collins and Jerry Porras, the authors of one of my favorite business books "Good to Great," called a "Big, Hairy, Audacious Goal." You'll normally see that referred to as a "BHAG." BHAGs are goals so big, hairy, and audacious that you don't quite know how you're going to achieve them.

A few years ago, I set a BHAG to do an Ironman Triathlon. For those who may not know what that entails, it's an endurance race that includes a 2.4-mile swim, a 112-mile bike ride, and a 26.2-mile run. When I set that goal, I knew what all the events were. I didn't know how much training I'd need or how my training needs would change. I set smaller, achievable goals and changed my goals as my fitness improved. I could never have planned it all in advance. I had to plan a little, then get started and change my goals as I went.

You might set a BHAG as achieving a major industry award, designation, or accreditation. You'll have to do many things to get there, usually for a long time. But when you start, you don't know all the specifics. That's okay. You'll work things out along the way.

Think of it like taking a major cross-country road trip. You're going to go from Phoenix to Boston. Along the way, you'll take some side trips and change your route a few times. But you keep moving toward Boston.

BHAGs should be inspiring. People should think, "That will be really something when we achieve that." Some writers call this your "Big Why." It reminds everyone of why what they're doing is important.

"Outcome goals" are the business goals we set for the month, the quarter, and the year. You set outcome goals for things like enrollment or performance against budget. They measure the outcome of activity.

Your outcome goals should be specific. Everyone should be able to tell if you've achieved the goal. Goals expert Stephen Lynch calls that the "pop the cork moment." There should be a time component. A key word is "by." For example, your goal may be to increase enrollment 50 percent "by" August 31."

Marjorie Blanchard calls outcome goals "a dream with a deadline." Every outcome goal you set should have both: a dream and a deadline.

Your short-term goals can include number of children enrolled, decreased staff turnover, and similar things. Be realistic but ambitious in setting your goals.

Consider behavioral goals. These measure activities you must do to achieve your short-term goals. For example, what do you need to do every day, week, or month to increase the number of children enrolled? Some centers have a staff member walk the family out to the parking lot at the end of the day, or offer a weekly game/activity to be excited about, or have a monthly theme.

Many people like the SMART Goal framework. SMART is an acronym that stands for Specific, Measurable, Achievable, Relevant, and Time-based. Each element of the SMART framework works together to create a goal that is carefully planned, clear, and trackable.

You don't want too many goals. In theory, one goal could cover everything. That's usually not possible, but the more goals you have the harder it is to achieve all of them. Most people seem to do best with a few outcome goals. And make sure every goal is realistic.

Stress-Testing Your Ideas

I mentioned Strategic Coach a moment ago. They provide lots of advice, but they also provide many forms that can help you be more effective. One of my favorites is The Impact Filter™, a one-page form that helps you define a project and clarify the project's goals and importance. I created an Impact Filter to help me decide whether or not to write this book. We use this tool regularly at my company, Menlo Group, to help make sound decisions.

The Impact Filter™ is a powerful tool to clarify and focus your thinking. Use it to sketch out your thinking and get really clear on your idea before you share it with others. It truly is a filter. You may realize after completing The Impact Filter™ that you're not sold on the idea, that it doesn't make a big enough impact to change how you're doing things now, or that the timing isn't right. By investing fifteen to twenty minutes to think through your idea at the beginning, you'll save far more time than if you don't.

It's also extremely useful in teamwork. The more clearly you communicate your intentions, the less you have to focus on managing, because everyone can get aligned with the results you're looking for.

The Impact Filter™ is one way to stress-test your idea. Here's another way.

Gabriele Oettingen is a psychology professor at New York University. For more than twenty years she's researched the role that positive thinking or imagining a successful outcome has on whether people achieve their goals.

She also developed a simple way to stress test your goal. The formal name is "mental contrasting," but I like the acronym better. It's WOOP. Here are the steps.

Wish: Think about what you want and why.

Objective: Sharpen that wish into a specific goal. Dream by deadline.

Obstacles: What can keep you from achieving your goal?

Plan: How will you deal with the obstacle? Think, "If X happens, then I'll do Y." The key is the "if-then" statement.

If your goal is realistic, you'll come up with ways to overcome each obstacle. That makes your plan better and gives you inspiration to pursue your goal. If you can't think of ways to deal with obstacles, you know that you should abandon the goal or change it so it's realistic.

Outcome goals are important, but they have one important flaw. You can only measure them after you've achieved them or not. They don't do a lot to help you get important work done every day.

The goals that will help you do something about your results go by various names. Sometimes they're called "lead indicators" because you assume that your performance on these goals will give you a good result when you get the reports on your outcome goals. Some writers call these "behavioral" goals because they measure activity, not outcome. And many of us call them "Key Performance Indicators" or KPIs.

Before that, though, we'll discuss two simple plans most centers use. Your marketing plan and budget both give you an overview of what you're trying to do and how successful you are. We'll start with the marketing plan.

Creating a Marketing Plan

One ***of the great cinematic events*** in my young life was the 1990 movie *Home Alone*. In the movie, young Kevin gets left behind when his family goes to Paris for Christmas. After he overheard two burglars (Marv and Harry) planning to burglarize his parent's home, rather than hide under the bed, Kevin jumped into action. He planned and executed a series of booby traps to defeat (and humiliate) Marv and Harry.

He poured water on the stairs, which would turn to ice and make the burglars slip and fall. He rigged buckets of paint so that when one of the burglars opened the door to the home's cellar, a full can of paint slammed into his head. For more than thirty years this movie has been a family favorite, especially during the holidays. I can't help but laugh when I think about it.

I laugh, but there's a serious lesson. Kevin did a great job of planning his booby traps and making them work. If you want to be as successful as Kevin in executing your plan, here's what you must do.

This is not a graduate-level course on how to do a marketing plan. There are books filled with advice on how-to's for that. You don't need to be an expert marketer or an expert planner, but you must know just enough about planning to know the important things to do and then have the discipline to do them.

I want to give you a high-level overview of creating a marketing plan. Here's a brief outline of what should be in it.

Mission Statement: Your mission statement outlines your business's values and services. This statement must be authentic. It should represent you and your brand accurately.

Know Your Audience: In order to best market to your audience, you need to know who they are. Develop an avatar that represents your ideal client. Once you have a good profile of who your target audience is, you can draft a strategy to reach them.

Services: In order to adequately market your services and your center, you need to be able to describe them. Take an inventory of the services you currently offer. Keep a running list of services you could offer.

Competitive Analysis: With a smartphone in every hand, your business faces a market that is more competitive than ever before. You need to do a competitive analysis to understand what others in your market are doing and find ways to differentiate yourself.

Marketing Strategy: This is where you outline how you will send the message of your value proposition to the people most likely to become clients.

Marketing Goals: A successful marketing plan is one with goals in mind.

Some Notes About Preparing Your Plan

When you see a list of the parts of a marketing plan, like what was just mentioned, you'll be tempted to think of putting it together as a nice, neat process. It's not. The result is neat, but the process is messy. Here's how to get the best results.

Concentrate on the three most important things. They're your avatar, your services, and your competition. These three are the core. If you get them right it's easy to write your mission statement, marketing strategy, and goals.

Look at the diagram below. Your avatar, services, and competition are each separate elements, but they're connected by arrows that point in both directions. That's because each thing you do in one should get you considering whether you need to change something in the other two.

YOUR AVATAR

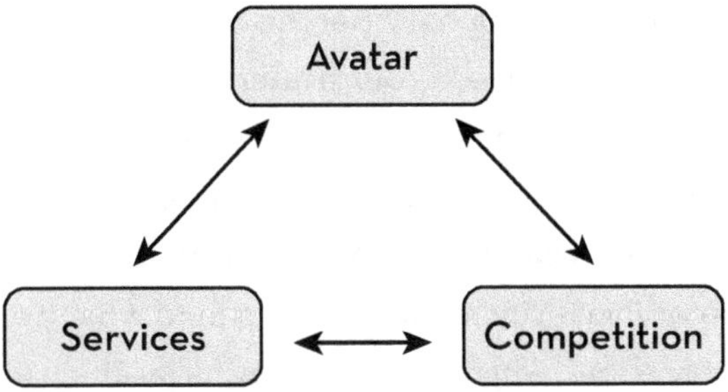

Avatar

Services

Competition

For example, you might decide that your avatar is a family where all the adults work. Thinking about that may spark the idea to offer extended hours to allow parents to pick up their children without stressful rushing. Or you might create a "rapid check out" process through your smartphone so when parents and/or loved ones arrive the "paperwork" is done. When you start analyzing that, you'll think to check the competition to see if any of your competitors offer these services. That may get you thinking about other services that may attract your avatar's business.

You'll continue this process over a couple of days, perhaps even a couple of weeks. Set it aside to let the unconscious part of your brain keep working while you do other things. You'll get ideas. Make sure to capture them.

Continue this process until you're done. So, how will you know when that is? You're done when your changes make things different but not necessarily better. I know that doesn't sound specific, but trust me, I think you'll know it when it happens.

Your Avatar

Your avatar is an imaginary person or family who will use your childcare services. Your avatar should be like a real person who would be your ideal customer. Demographic descriptions of age, gender, and location are great, but they're not the whole story. You want to understand how your avatar lives. You want to understand what he, she, or they worry about, what problems they have—the pain points in their life. That's emotional, not statistical.

Try writing the description of a typical day for your avatar. What time do they get up? What's their morning routine like? What's their commute like and where would they prefer to drop their children for childcare?

Imagine your avatar having a conversation with a friend and talking about childcare. Why will they say they're considering it? What are they concerned about? What do they want from a childcare provider?

Right now, you're probably thinking, "Sure, but there are so many different people that can be my customer, not just one."

You're right. So, don't limit yourself to a single avatar. You can have two, three, or four as you work through a good description. You'll find several commonalities that will clearly define your final avatar. When you're done, you should have a clear picture in your head of the ideal person who will use the services you provide. You'll use that knowledge when you craft your value proposition.

Your Services

The second key element is services. That starts with your avatar's expectations.

No matter what services you offer or where you're located, there are some basic things your potential clients will expect. They will expect you to meet current licensing and other requirements. They will expect you to provide a clean and safe environment for their children. They will expect you to communicate with them and treat them with respect.

You don't list any of those things in your marketing materials. They're called "hygiene factors." Having a clean and safe environment, for example, won't influence a client to choose your childcare operation over another one. But if you don't have a clean and safe environment, you're likely to be eliminated from consideration right away.

Hygiene factors are what parents expect every childcare center to have. If you don't have them, it doesn't matter what else you do. Make a list of the things every parent expects from every childcare center and make sure you meet those expectations.

Your services are how you set yourself apart from other childcare centers. What is it that you do especially well? How are you different and distinctive?

Tom Hall and his partner grew Ensslin and Hall Advertising into one of the country's top regional agencies in less than a decade. The core of their success was the question Tom asked every new client at their first meeting: "What do you want to be known for?"

What do you want to be known for? What's the service that's at the heart of your childcare center? Those are the things to consider when you craft your value proposition.

Your Competition

Compare yourself to other childcare centers in the market. Analyze who competes with you for the same clients and how the two of you compare. Probably the simplest form of competitive analysis is called a SWOT analysis. SWOT stands for strengths, weaknesses, opportunities, and threats.

What are your strengths? What do you do especially well that sets you apart from your competition? You might offer a curriculum with special benefits. You might offer extended hours or special kinds of meals. Identify your own strengths but take the extra step of analyzing the strengths of all the competitors you can identify.

Weaknesses are the flipside of your strengths. Most people think that what you do once you've found a weakness is to eliminate it. That's one possible strategy. Your overall goal should be to make your weakness irrelevant. You can do that by either learning to do whatever your weakness is well enough or diminishing the importance of the weakness. Look for ways to turn your weakness to your advantage. Is there a way to present your "weakness" in a way that appeals to potential clients?

Opportunities are where you identify something in the market you can exploit. Look for gaps in the offerings of your competitors. What can you do that makes you both different from and better than your competition?

Don't forget threats. Ask yourself what your competitors could do that would give them the advantage. Consider other threats like area growth or development, potential age gaps in your area, or large employers that might be coming or going from your area.

SWOT ANALYSIS (EXAMPLE)

Strengths	Weaknesses
• Location • Brand New Building • Curriculum • Experienced Staff	• Staff Turnover • No Room to Grow • Small Employment Base
Opportunities	**Threats**
• New Programs • Expansion • Growing Area	• Competition • People Working from Home • Increase in Wages

So far, we've talked about the competition with other childcare centers. But childcare centers aren't your only competition. You compete with grandparents who provide childcare for their grandchildren. You may compete with an afterschool program at a local church or community center. You certainly compete with the stay-at-home parent who provides childcare as part of what he or she does. Think of your indirect competition as anything a child from your target group might do regularly instead of coming to your center.

Work out the details of your avatar, your services, and your competition. Pay attention to how changes in one affect the other two.

Your Value Proposition

Your value proposition is your main promise to clients and prospective clients. It's how you tell them what they can expect from you. It's what guides your choices about which services you deliver and how you deliver them.

Write out your value proposition in a sentence or two. When you do, consider the following.

What makes you different? Is your big promise rooted in your curriculum? Maybe your big promise is in your general approach to life. Maybe your big promise is about making things easier for working parents. Whatever it is it should be the core of your value proposition.

The big promise is the positive side of your proposition. Very often, the best way to describe your big promise is to talk about the things that won't be true anymore. For example, you might offer extended care hours that remove the worry about fighting traffic to get to the center on time. If you offer technological ways for parents to observe their child, you also eliminate worrying about their child while they're at work.

No matter what value you offer, if you're asking people to change either from caring for their children themselves or from another childcare center, expect them to be nervous about the new choice. You can use examples of other people who made a similar choice and received a great childcare experience for their child and themselves. Remember, the easiest thing for a person to do is just to keep doing what they're doing now. Give them a powerful reason to change.

Your Marketing Strategy

There are many options to choose from when determining your marketing strategy. There are many advertising/marketing companies out there willing to take your money. Be prudent in the beginning. Ask your staff and advisors for ideas. This is a trial-and-error process that you will never be done with and that will never be 100 percent accurate. But you must start somewhere.

There's no limit to the number of things you can try. Here are a few of them.

Today, people search for everything on the web. Make sure you have a website. The web address should appear on all your digital and printed material, along with your name, address, and phone number.

Create a page on Facebook, Instagram, and other social media platforms.

Make sure people can find your website on Google and Google Maps.

Create a flyer or a brochure you can leave with prospective clients and in places people with children visit. Examples are family fun centers, popular restaurants, and movie theaters.

Consider mailing to families like your avatar. Postcards are a highly effective alternative to letters.

As you develop relationships with clients, ask them for testimonials. Use the testimonials on your digital and printed material.

Encourage clients, family, and friends to refer people to you.

Be active in the community. Talk to people about your center.

This is just a start. You and your team can come up with many more ways to let potential clients know about you. There are lots of right answers to how to market your center. Every center is different. What works for another center may not work for you. Here's how a few experts do it.

Tym Smith

I've got a wonderful location with fantastic curb appeal, and it's great. But I also have a couple of centers that are tucked back behind other businesses, and you would have no idea that they're there unless you knew that they were there. So, marketing is a big piece of this. Of course, the best thing you can do is word of mouth. There is nothing better than word of mouth and making your families your marketing partners.

Barbie Prinster

The other thing that people don't really realize about preschools is the marketing is your parents. Your parents go to soccer games, your parents go to softball games, your parents go to swim lessons, and they talk.

So, I think it's about building those relationships, and at the same time, we used to do mailers and things like that, but I really think the social media piece is probably the bigger piece right now for marketing.

Alissa Thompson

I'm not very good at social media, so my marketing was a lot of pounding pavement, honestly. Like, I made door hangers, I went to all the apartment complexes in the area. I had somebody stand on the corner with a sign. A lot of my marketing strategies were kind of old-fashioned.

Elana Hillel

We actually hired a marketing firm that specializes in childcare.

Your Marketing Goals

Set marketing goals the same way you set other goals. You'll have both outcome goals and behavioral goals. Your outcome goals should measure your results for the last month, quarter, or year. Your behavioral goals should describe the actions you should take every day, week, or month if you want to achieve your outcome goals.

A good marketing plan describes how you'll tell the world about your childcare center. It helps you fill your center with happy customers with many more on the waiting list. In the next chapter, you'll learn about how to create a business plan that will guide your operations and improve your odds of getting funding when, or if, you need it.

Creating and Using a Budget

I'*m sure you're passionate* about your childcare business, so let me be blunt. You must be disciplined enough to make the time to understand the financial aspects of your business. Otherwise, you'll have no business to be passionate about.

You may be one of those people who breaks out in hives when you think about finance, accounting, or creating a budget. But if you want to have a successful childcare center, having a general understanding of accounting is important. Accounting isn't a success factor. A great accounting system won't help you become a profitable center. But many centers have gone under despite having great programs and passionate staff because they didn't take the time to become educated on how to pay attention to the numbers.

Remember the woman we talked about in the Due Diligence chapter? She had plenty of money. And she probably thought she didn't need to pay attention to the details because she could always "buy" her way out of trouble. That's not what happened. She had plenty of money, but no discipline, and in the end, she didn't have a childcare business either.

That woman was very different from a client I worked with several years ago. She was director of a center for many years and had other jobs in the industry. She waited for the right opportunity to start her own center. While she was waiting, she planned and saved until the right opportunity came along. Then she did what was necessary to make it successful.

She doesn't *like* accounting. But she knew she needed strong financial statements to get the kind of funding she needed to start up. And she knows that paying attention to her financials helps her stay on top of the business, meet inevitable challenges, and head off unforeseen situations that can and do arise.

What I want to do in this chapter is cover some of the basics so you can "speak accounting" to potential business partners, lenders, and or investors. You don't have to become an accountant, but you need to know enough about the numbers to communicate with lenders and manage the profitability of your center effectively.

When we've covered the basics, I'll show you how you can put them together to understand how your business works. We'll build on that so you can obtain funding when you need it, spot money problems early, and manage them effectively.

Some Things You Must Know

There are a few definitions and concepts you should know if you want to know enough about accounting to manage your center. Here are a few of them.

Bookkeeping Equation

The bookkeeping equation is simple, and so is the concept behind it. Here's the equation:

Profit = Revenue—Expenses

You want to have profit left after you've paid all the expenses for a month or a quarter or a year. There's only two ways you can make profit go up. You can increase revenue, or you can decrease expenses. Over time, you'll be profitable if you consistently work to build revenue and control expenses.

That's important because many childcare operators concentrate on either revenue or expenses. They try to keep expenses down without paying attention to the revenue. Or they put all their effort into filling up the center with children without paying attention to expenses.

Profit and Loss Statement (P&L)

A profit and loss statement, or P&L, records the activity for a period of time. That period might be a month or a quarter or a year. On the P&L, you count up all the revenue you've received and then subtract all the expenses you've paid. The result is either profit or loss. This is also called an "Income Statement."

Balance Sheet

A balance sheet is a financial snapshot of the financial condition of the business at a particular point in time. It shows your assets, which is everything you own, including cash. It shows your liabilities, which is everything you owe. The statement also shows your equity. Equity is what you have left after you liquidate all your assets and pay all your liabilities. The equation looks like this:

Assets = Liabilities + Equity

Cash Flow

You pay your basic operating expenses with cash. You need cash to pay for things like salaries. It won't do to have money that's "coming in, someday." You need the cash when it's time to make payroll. A cash flow statement helps you stay on top of whether you will have the cash to meet your obligations.

Pro Forma

When you deal with lenders or other investors, they will probably ask you for a "*pro forma*" statement. *Pro formas* are statements you use to share your expected financial results. A *pro forma* statement is a statement of future results based on certain assumptions.

Fixed Costs and Variable Costs

I've seen childcare operators get in trouble because they didn't understand the difference. Fixed costs are the costs you pay regardless of how many children you have enrolled or what season of the year it is. Fixed costs can include your rent or mortgage. Here's Ted Batycki:

> *Our industry has a lot of fixed costs that are not as elastic to demand. So, the cost of electricity and the cost of liability insurance and property taxes, those are all the same whether I have twenty children in a building or two hundred children in the building.*

Variable costs vary depending on your level of activity. If you increase your enrollment, you're likely to increase your food and supplies expenses. When enrollment declines, so do variable costs.

Those are some basic definitions you'll need to know so you can "speak accounting" when necessary. The definitions are important, but they're not enough for you to deal with lenders and manage your center effectively.

You Need a Professional Advisor

It's important for you to know something about how to manage your center's finances. But don't try to do it alone. You need help to deal with the different laws, regulations, and financial situations you will encounter.

An accountant should be one of your key professional advisors. He or she will make sure your accounting meets necessary requirements and your taxes are filed on time. For many center operators, an accountant is also a source of financial and general business advice.

If you're affiliated with a national company, you will have access to information that will help you manage your finances. Take some time to find out what resources are available.

Use your friends in the business as a personal help desk. Tap into their experiences for insight, information, and ideas.

Creating a Basic Operating Budget

The budget is the financial statement you will use the most. A budget is your basic plan for how things will go for the next month, quarter, or year. It's a planning document.

Your budget is also a tool that you'll compare to actual results to see how you're doing. That will help you spot problems early and determine what action to take. It's a management document.

Count all your sources of income. They include your tuition and income from fees, such as late payment or late pickup.

Now consider all the things you'll have to spend money on. Start with what you'll spend on people. Include salaries and payroll taxes. Include any amounts you'll spend on contractors. Include worker's compensation and any benefits.

List all your other expenses. It may help you to do several lists at different times and compare them. Talk to your advisors and friends who are in the business. Ask them if you've missed anything.

This is a good time to mark each of your expenses as fixed or variable. If you're in doubt, ask yourself if you would pay this expense whether or not you have any children enrolled.

I can't stress this enough. Have a solid source for every figure you put into the budget. If you've been in business for a while, you can use some of your historical information. Otherwise, you need to get some numbers that are likely to be accurate.

The Risk Management Association (RMA) publishes *pro forma* statements for many kinds of businesses. You or your accountant can get these statements and use them as sources for several line items. They'll also help you check to see if you have included all reasonable sources of income and all reasonable expenses.

When you get to items like food, don't use your "best guess." Instead, talk to your food vendor to see what he or she says you're likely to be charged. Talk to other center operators and find out what their experience is.

There are childcare budgets you can find online. You can use them as a starting point, but make sure the figures you enter reflect what you expect for your center. Here's advice from Heather Torres of Hope Lutheran Learning Center:

> *You can't simply take the amount you spent on utilities and divide it by twelve and apply that number across the months. Depending on where you live, you may spend more on utilities in the summer. At our center, the amount we spend on salaries also increases in the summer. Well, why is that? Because we have a*

summer program that I hire more teachers for. I also have more income because I have more students in the summer months.

Your budget should be as realistic as you can make it. Your budget is a simplified financial plan. It will be the financial document that guides your operations from week to week.

Understand the Basics of How Your Business Works

Let's start with a hard truth. It's hard to make a profit in childcare, but you'll increase your odds of success if you take the time to understand how your business works.

Spend some time and take a basic bookkeeping course. There are several available at local community colleges, night schools, and online. It's the best way I know to get a basic understanding of how accounting works.

Ask your accountant to help you understand the financial workings of your center. He or she can probably set up a simple spreadsheet that will help you understand how one thing affects another in your business. What expenses do you incur when you add one student to your enrollment? What happens when a staff member is ready for a raise? What if your food vendor's pricing changes?

Understand How to Keep Up with How You're Doing

Savvy childcare operators pay attention to their finances. When you do that, you can spot problems early, when they're easier to solve. And you can use your finances to analyze how to make the right changes.

Review your budget regularly. Regularly means at least once a week. If you spot an issue that doesn't seem right, try to figure it out yourself. If you can't or if you want someone to check your work, talk to your professional advisor.

Keep up with your regular accounting entries so you can compare reality with your budget. Use your regular review of your planned budget versus your actual financial performance to spot things that call for action or more work to understand. The key to using your budget effectively is consistency. Consistently make your accounting entries. Review your budget consistently.

Keeping up with your accounting can sharpen your awareness of how your business is working. Keeping up with your accounting will help you make better projections in the future. When you review your budget regularly, you'll catch problems early, and you'll have information that will help you solve them.

This chapter introduced you to some basic accounting, finance, and budgeting concepts and how to create a budget that can also be a simple planning tool. In this section, you've learned about the basics of business planning and how it can be the difference between success and failure.

In the next section, you'll learn about effective childcare center operations.

SECTION 3

Details of Running Your Center

T*his section is about the moments of truth* in childcare. Everything we discussed so far—all the values, planning, funding, location-finding, budgeting, and marketing—is put to the test when you begin caring for children. The Details of Running Your Center Section has three chapters to help make your vision of success a reality.

The first chapter in the section is "Hiring the Right People." If you hire the right people, support them, and treat them fairly, you almost assure success. Several of the people I interviewed thought hiring and supervising was the hardest part of running a childcare center.

"Management and Operations" is the second chapter in this section. What you and your staff do every day determines the success or failure of your center. You'll learn about distributing the work so everything important gets done properly. You'll discover how to run effective meetings, compute cost of care, and supervise effectively.

The final chapter in this section and the book is "Your Building." The design of your space affects the quality of care you can provide and the profitability of your center. You'll learn how to assemble a team and create processes, so you can deliver the best care possible. Parents use their impressions of your building as an important factor when they decide whether they want to send their child to your center. You'll discover how to make that work for you. Finally, you'll learn how to do effective maintenance, so you stay ahead of licensing problems.

Hiring the Right People

M*any management writers talk* about the importance of people in their organizations. In his book, *Good to Great*, Jim Collins uses a bus analogy. He says that you must get the right people in the right seats on the bus before you can drive the bus anywhere.

Dan Sullivan, founder and president of Strategic Coach, has written an entire book on the subject called *Who Not How*. One of my favorite ways to express the thought is in the blunt words of Walter Wriston, who was the chair and CEO of Citibank: "If you have good people in the right spots, there's almost nothing you can do to screw it up."

That's because people are the way you deliver your value proposition. You may have an amazing curriculum, but the people on your team bring it to life for the children. You may believe in the abstract that taking time to talk with parents is a good idea, but someone must actually take that time and have those conversations.

Not only is hiring the right people important, it's also hard. Alissa Thompson shares her experience:

I think finding the right people is the absolute hardest thing. For the first six months, I spun my wheels big time when it came to staff. I never met so many flighty, unreliable people in my life. But you get to a point where you find those few cores, and then they know people, and those people know more people, and before long, you are bringing people in with experience.

This chapter is about getting the right people in the right seats. We'll start by talking about what work needs to be done and how you figure out who the right people are. We'll talk about core values and an effective, structured hiring process. We'll wrap up this chapter with a look at how helping people grow makes your center the place where great people want to stay.

What Needs to Be Done

Creating an environment where great people can do great work starts with knowing what needs to be done. If you know what needs to be done to make your center run, then you can choose the people best suited to doing the job.

As part of this process, you should talk to your experts and people you know in the industry. Every childcare center is unique, but all childcare centers must do certain kinds of things to succeed. Those things generally fall into four buckets: operations, finance and accounting, human resources, and sales and marketing.

Operations includes all the things you must do to make your center run effectively. Operations covers basic childcare functions. It also includes basic administrative functions and mundane, daily tasks like locking and unlocking the doors.

Finance and accounting are the things that you do to manage your money. Finance and accounting includes creating and managing the budget. It also includes filing taxes in a timely manner and making sure you have good cashflow.

Human Resources include the things you do related to hiring and firing people. HR functions include drawing up specific job descriptions. It also includes helping people grow and develop, so the right people want to stay with you forever.

Sales and marketing include everything you do that makes potential clients aware of you, interested in you, and finally, become a client. Most people who write about marketing see marketing as the things you do when you're addressing a larger audience. You build recognition. You make people aware of what you do. When they become interested, you answer their specific questions and address their specific concerns.

Make lists of everything that must be done in each of these four areas. Talk to your experts, such as your accountant, for their opinions. Talk to people you know in the industry.

As I've suggested with other lists in this book, don't make your list all at one time. Work on it over a period of several days or weeks, adding things as you think of them. Taking your time increases the likelihood that good ideas will bubble up from your brain. It also gives you time to talk to different experts and experienced childcare operators.

In the beginning, you may have to do almost everything. That's normal. As time goes on, though, you'll want to hire quality people to do the work. Sometimes, it'll make sense to outsource the work. For instance, many centers outsource payroll. Many also hire a janitorial services firm to clean the center.

Your goal is to have the right people doing every important task. So, let's think about who those "right people" might be.

The Right People

There's a story lots of motivational speakers like to tell. It involves someone (often a historical personage) walking by workers where a grand cathedral is being built. The personage asks three stonemasons in succession what they're doing. The first one replies, "I'm cutting stone." The second one replies, "I'm trying to be the best stonemason in the world." Finally, the third stonemason says, "I'm helping build a great cathedral."

For most motivational speakers, the moral of that tale is that you want to hire the people who are thinking about something bigger than they are. They're the ones who want to build the great cathedral. I agree with that, but with one reservation. I think all those people who want to be part of building a great cathedral also ought to be people who are trying to do their best work.

The right people for a childcare center are team players. Childcare is a team effort, and everyone on the team is important.

The right people are also people who understand and adopt your core values. Your core values define your purpose. Tym Smith goes a little further. He likes to say,

What you're hiring for isn't a job; it's a purpose.

You've probably heard of companies' core values and value statements. Often, they're just plaques on the wall or words on a website. Those aren't the kind of core values I'm talking about. The core values I'm talking about motivate and inspire every member of your team and affects everything they do and say.

Sometimes, your core values will help you make a tough choice. One of the core values at Ted Batycki's center is,

What's right for the children is what's right for our business.

I'm sure that, like every childcare center owner, he thinks of different ways to do things that would save some money. It's tempting to do that without thinking about the consequences. Ted can use his core values to ask if the particular action is good for the children. If it is, he can make the choice and save some money. But if it isn't, adhering to core values helps Ted run the kind of center he wants to run.

It's important for you to define your core values. That's not an easy process or a quick one. Ted Batycki says that when he and his wife wrote their first set of core values, it took them about six weeks. The process involves writing something out, letting it rest, reviewing it, and revising it. You do that until everything seems to fit.

Your values come into play in many different areas. Martha Picciao from Whiz Kidz uses her center's core values to check decisions. They might ask, "Are we putting our families first if we do this?" If a core value is caring for staff, she might ask if an additional program would add to the workload too much.

Later, when your staff has been at work for a while and has tried to live your core values, you can follow Ted's example and rewrite the core values as a group.

One of the most important things that core values can do for you is help you make hiring decisions. Elana Hillel from Premiere Learning Academy uses core values to help with hiring decisions. Here are her thoughts:

> *When you come in for an interview, if you don't meet any of our core values, you're not hired. I don't care if you were a teacher for twenty-five years.*

Core values should not be "one and done." If they're going to be a living statement of what drives your center, you should review them and revise them regularly if necessary. I suggest you do that as part of your annual business planning. The leadership team in our organization reviews our core values quarterly.

Hiring

People you hire become part of your center's team. That should be good for them and for you. If you want to have great people on your team, you must be able to answer "Yes" to all three questions:

- Will this person commit to our core values?
- Will this person do excellent work?
- Will this person thrive in our center?

It will be tempting to hire people where there are only one or two yeses. That's only one of the great temptations in hiring.

You'll be tempted to hire someone to fill a position without paying attention to overall qualifications and fit. That temptation will be especially strong if the position has been open for a while and if other team members are having to do extra work to cover. Don't fall into this trap. In most cases, you'll be better off with an overworked team of the right people than with a team where one or more people don't fit.

Sadly, many people are better at interviewing than they are at the jobs they're interviewing for. These people make such a good impression that you'll want to hire them right away. Don't succumb to that temptation. Follow a thorough, structured process to make good hires and follow the same process every time.

Following a good hiring process every time can help you make more good hires. Here's a process that has worked for many organizations.

List your must-haves and nice-to-haves. What items are absolutely essential? You won't hire anybody who doesn't have these qualifications or that experience. What would be a plus, a nice-to-have? Knowing these things gives you a rough idea of the kind of person you want to wind up with.

Use structured interviews. Structured interviews ask every candidate the same questions in the same order. With a structured interview, you make sure you're covering all the bases. Structured interviews also give you an easy way to compare candidates.

I suggest a two-person interview for the first interview with a candidate. One person functions as the interviewer. He or she asks the questions in the structured interview. The other person acts as the recorder. He or she makes notes about how the interview goes, when the candidate seemed engaged and when he or she seemed uncomfortable. The recorder should also take down the questions that the candidate asks. Those questions can tell you quite a bit about a possible fit with your values.

I don't think it's a good idea to hire based on a single interview. I recommend at least three. Two or more of those can be team interviews. In a team interview, the people the candidate will work with conduct the interview. They should have a couple of specific questions they want to ask and go into the interview with an idea of what they're looking for.

When you're done with the interviews, check references on anyone you're thinking about hiring. Do not skip this step. If possible, talk with the person who was the candidate's supervisor. Ask about their quality of work, motivation, and how the person worked as part of a team. At the end of the interview, ask the reference who else would know the candidate well enough to answer some questions.

A good, thorough interview process takes time, but it should result in people who will be more productive and stay longer. In early childhood, many interviewees are young with little to no work experience, and their references can include church/youth leaders, coaches, and teachers. Ask for people who know their character. Remember, you are hiring in line with core values.

Talk with your attorney about whether you should have employees sign an employment contract. They can be helpful if you use the contract to outline what you expect in terms of working up to your values and reasons for termination. As an employer, you're committing to providing a great place to work with fair compensation, great culture, and core values. In return, you're expecting commitment from the people you hire, and an employment contract is a great way of showing reciprocal commitment.

This is not a place for "do it yourself." Employment law and contract law limit what you can and cannot do. The precise wording of a contract is important to assure that the contract gets the results you want. Get expert help.

Onboarding

Onboarding is the process of bringing someone into your center and helping both of you learn if you have a good fit. Too many centers leave this to chance.

Plan the first couple of days for the new hire in detail. Commit time to help them learn about your center and how you do things.

A good onboarding process does two things. It helps you learn about the new hire. And it helps that new hire learn about you and become more productive quickly. Too many places don't plan the onboarding process. The new hire winds up standing around killing time while the person who's supposedly helping them learn about the center attends to something else.

The first few days are critical to helping the new hire feel like they've made the right decision joining your team. Make sure your existing team knows to go out of their way to make them feel welcome.

Plan each day from open to close. You may want to have some individual activity and group activity. You might hand off the person to another person for different parts of the day. Take care to make the entire process helpful and interesting.

You may decide that your onboarding process needs more than a few days. Here's how Elana Hillel extends the process at her center.

> *So, what we do is we interview candidates for two weeks before they're hired as pretend teachers. And then, once they're hired, we have a strict ninety-day onboarding process, and they're only hired as floaters, which are substitute teachers. No one is ever hired as a teacher at our preschool. So, you'll always shadow someone for three months until we decide if you're made for it.*

Helping People Grow

Most people, especially the "right" people, don't just want to show up and do good work. They want to get better at things each and every day. They want to make personal progress. That's why it's important for you to pay attention to their learning.

Some of their learning may be mandatory. Sometimes, you'll select training for the entire group that you want them to attend. That's important.

People learn on the job in another way, too. Provide the people who work for you with coaching so that each day they get a bit better.

There's another kind of learning and growth that goes by the name "action learning." In action learning, people participate in a problem-solving team to make things better at work. They're part of a team of two or three other people attacking a specific problem for your center. Offer these as learning opportunities.

It's tempting to offer many learning opportunities without considering the value. Tym Smith says:

> *Every dime that you spend on that employee and their professional development, you should be getting a return on that investment.*

The people who work at your center are the people who will determine the success or failure of your center. Make sure you know what needs to be done. Look for people who will do excellent work and commit to your core values. Hire them using a structured process that will help you avoid common hiring temptations. Then, help them do good work. The next chapter on running your center will introduce you to some tools that will help the people at your center perform at their best.

Management and Operations

When I was growing up, I was a Scout. First a Cub Scout, then a Boy Scout, and finally an Eagle Scout. As I got older, I had the opportunity to volunteer with several Scout troops in my church assignments in my community.

I was asked to coordinate a fundraiser for one of the troops. We were organizing a fundraiser breakfast. How hard could it be to coordinate it all? If you've ever done something like that, you know the answer. It's a lot more work with a lot more details than you could possibly imagine beforehand.

We expected two hundred to three hundred people. We had to coordinate a location with sufficient tables and chairs, make up a menu, and purchase and serve the food. We needed a system to account for funds. All the Scouts involved needed something to do. Oh yes, we also needed to distribute the leftovers and clean up.

One big problem was that I needed to figure everything out, as if it had never been done before. It would have been far easier for me if there were some checklists or notes about how a fundraiser breakfast is to be done.

I've experienced a similar concept in working with childcare centers. When there's a task to be done, too often the task is reinvented again and again. There's no systems or processes in place.

You want to spend as much time as possible on childcare. You don't want to spend hours every week figuring out how to do basic management tasks.

In this chapter, you'll learn how to use an organization chart and lists of various kinds to make sure your center is a well-oiled machine. You'll also learn a powerful technique to make sure that things get done properly. You'll learn how to have productive meetings, too. We'll wrap up the chapter with a discussion of how you can make your center a place where the right people want to work.

Your Organization Chart

I'm sure you've seen an organization chart. There's a box up at the top that's labeled something like "CEO" or "Owner." Below it are boxes representing the people and jobs that report to the CEO or owner. Below those boxes are more boxes. The people and jobs in those boxes report to those just above them. That's how we do it today, but the first organizational chart looked different.

It looked like a tree, with branches extending out from a central point and bearing fruit. The title was "Diagram Representing a Plan of Organization" for the New York and Erie Railroad. It was the brainchild of the General Superintendent of the railroad, David McCallum.

McCallum's chart and the ones we use today show all the jobs in an organization. The people who fill those jobs are responsible for doing the things in their job description. When you start your center, there may be only one box, the one with your name in it. At that point, you're responsible for everything, but since your center probably isn't operating yet, that won't be an issue. As your center grows and enrollment picks up, you'll add jobs and shift the tasks around.

Here's the basic principle. Every box on your chart represents a job and, usually, the person who holds the job. There should be a job description for every role describing the tasks that should be done. All the job descriptions together should cover all the work that needs to be done in your center. Start with the task lists you developed in the last chapter.

ORGANIZATION CHART

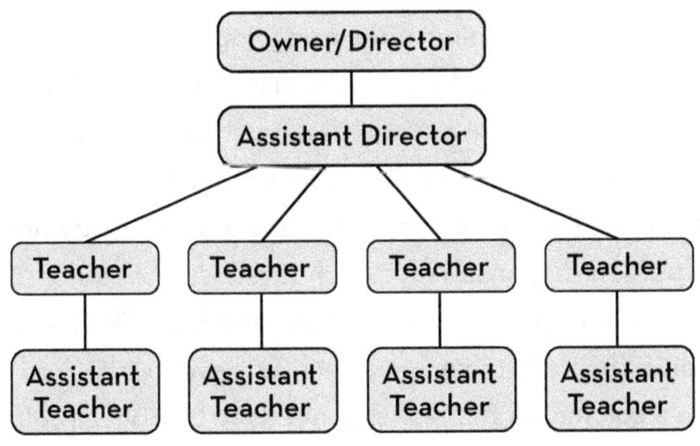

As you work through those task lists and assign them to different jobs, you will probably think of other things that should be done. Add them to the list and put them on a job description.

Make Sure Everything Important Gets Done

It's not enough to simply make lists of the tasks that must be done and assign them to particular jobs. You should also decide when each task should be done. The combination of what to do, when to do it, and who is responsible helps you stay on top of things.

One of the easiest tools to use is a recurring events list. The principle is that every task that needs to be done routinely should be done that way. You shouldn't have to think about it or plan for it every time. Then you free up mental energy you can use for other purposes. Recurring events lists help you do that.

I suggest recurring events lists that are daily, weekly, monthly, quarterly, and less often. Some things must be done every day, like opening and closing your center. There are other things that must be done every week, some that must be done every month, some that must be done quarterly, and some that need to be done less often. Put the tasks on the proper lists. Then, tie those lists to the jobs by noting the person responsible for each task.

Here's a tip. You can use a spreadsheet like Excel or Google Sheets to create your recurring events lists. You can have a column for the task that needs to be done, a column for the frequency, and a column for the person responsible.

Excel or Google Sheets makes it easy to sort the columns in various ways. You can sort them alphabetically by task, by which list they're on (daily, weekly, monthly), and by the person responsible.

You'll find it helpful if you also work with a reminder system that tells you when things need to be done. There are all kinds of physical reminder systems, from the very elaborate down to the person who just makes notes on his or her calendar. You'll find them described in books and articles on time management.

Since we're in the Digital Age, there are programs that can live on your computer, online, or your smartphone. Search for "reminder systems" or "task management systems." Two popular ones are Todoist and Remember the Milk. Both have apps so you can use their system on your smartphone.

Find out which systems your friends in the childcare industry use. That way, you'll find a program that you know works for people like you, and you'll have your more-experienced friends as a kind of built-in help desk.

So far, we've talked about making sure things get done by knowing when they need to be done and who should be responsible for them. That's crucial, but not enough. We must also make sure that everything is done properly.

Make Sure Things Get Done Properly

There's a lot to do and check before an airplane takes off. My mom was a flight attendant for almost thirty years. I spent lots of time in the cockpit when I was young. I loved watching my mom go through the safety checklists. I also became aware of the things the pilots needed to check before the plane took off.

Controls must be checked to see if they're operational. Gauges must be checked to assure there's fuel in the tanks. There are hundreds of things that need to be done on every flight. That's why pilots use checklists.

You may not be responsible for anything as technical as a jumbo jet, but your center has things that should be done in the same way every time. Checklists will help you do that without relying on your memory.

Checklists give you another benefit. The act of putting together a written checklist forces you to consider routine operations in detail. This is an excellent activity for several staff members. It pays to have more brains in the game. You're likely to get a more thorough list and better understanding of the sequence of the checklist when several people put it together.

You should put together checklists for all your basic activities. Here are some things to consider.

- Opening and closing the center
- Prospective parent visit or tour
- Parent visit

Here's an example of how one operator, Elana Hillel, uses a checklist.

Our checklist is actually the DHS checklist that inspectors use. So, when they come in, there's no surprises. They have a long list and a very short list of things to do, and we incorporate that into our daily, weekly, and monthly operations.

Elana's center uses the checklist as part of a morning walkthrough they do every day. In this case, it's tied to the regulations they need to comply with.

We can take another lesson from pilots here. Pilots have normal checklists for normal operations. That's what we've been talking about so far. But they also have "non-normal" checklists for special situations. These are usually emergencies. When you have a checklist for an emergency, you don't have to come up with a plan on the spot when stress levels are high. Here are some things you might create non-normal checklists for:

- A fire
- A child medical emergency
- A staff medical emergency
- An earthquake or other natural disaster common in your area

Collect the wisdom behind your checklists in binders for important recurring events. Create binders for inspections, insurance, parent visits, and other key matters.

Meetings

Meetings don't get much good press. Most people say they hate them, and they've got their reasons. If you're like me, meetings can sometimes be a not so fun trip to "snoozeville." Many meetings aren't necessary. Other meetings are poorly run, usually with one person talking and everyone else listening.

At my company we've invested in Traction Tools for EOS. They've developed some excellent tools for all aspects of a small business, including an excellent package that helps us run meetings that actually get things done. It helps you and your organization focus on the most important things and to make decisions and complete tasks efficiently and effectively.

When people are meeting, they're not working. Limit your meetings to those necessary for your organization and where several people must be in the room. Develop an email routine for information-sharing when coordination isn't important.

Think of how you communicate with three different groups of people. Imagine them as concentric circles.

MEETINGS

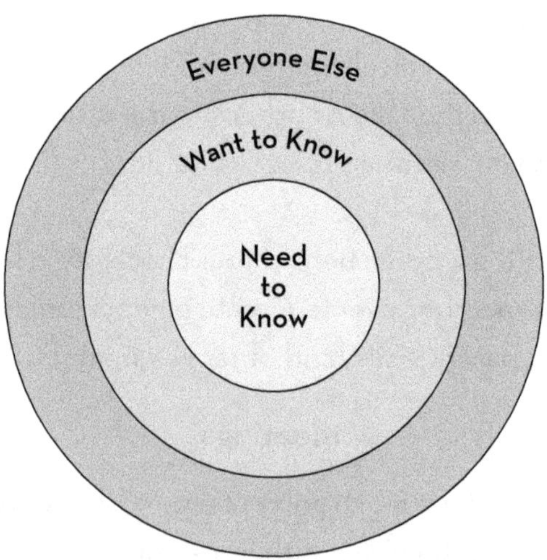

In the center ring are the people who need to know. Normally, those will be the people who attend a meeting. The next ring out are people who want to know. They've asked to be advised via email about what happens at the meeting. Send them meeting notes via email, text, instant messenger, etc. The final circle includes people in every other group. For them, meeting notes should go into a depository on your network or in a weekly reading file that's distributed to everyone.

Develop a regular meeting cadence with the same kinds of meetings at the same day and time every week or month. Simple group meetings to report on what people are doing and what help they need from others can be done as standups in a few minutes every day or every week.

Supervisors should also have one-on-ones with everyone who reports to them. The purpose of a one-on-one is to make sure people understand the work they're supposed to do and that they have adequate resources to do it. It's also to identify any other issues or desires they may have and discuss ways to support the person. This is a great opportunity for them to provide and ask for feedback. Everyone needs an avenue to feel heard and be heard.

Cost of Care

Do you know what it costs you to provide services to one child for one day? If you don't know the answer to that question, you're flying blind when you make decisions about tuition, space utilization, and much more.

You might require expert help to do a sophisticated cost of care analysis by program or to work out the time impact of different pricing strategies. But you should be aware of the concept.

To calculate the cost to provide services to one child for one day, you need to know the following:

- Total expenses for a year
- Enrollment
- The number of days the center is open

Then the math looks like this:

Total cost per child per day = Total expenses/enrollment/ number of days the center is open

Your cost of care may change if you change your staffing ratios. It may change if you change the way your physical space is set up. It *will* change if expenses or enrollment change.

There are more details on cost of care in the Appendix. As with due diligence, the most important thing to know about cost of care analysis is that you should do it. Here's Tym Smith on the value of cost of care.

> *Especially for brand-new directors and owners coming in, you need to go through the process of doing cost of care so that you can really see for each individual child, what your profit or loss is on that individual child.*

The Big Challenge

So far, it might seem that management is a mechanical process. Whether you are creating job descriptions, forms, or checklists, all are mechanical processes. Those are important, but management is a human process. Your challenge as an owner or director is to make your center a great place to work.

Think about the work. The people who work at your center should deliver your value proposition and focus on the fundamentals of your business.

Think about the people. Edward Deci and Richard Ryan have studied people at work for almost fifty years. They discovered a few critical things that people want from work. People want to make as many decisions as possible about their work. People want to do interesting work and get better at it. People want to work with people they like.

Interesting work shouldn't be a problem. People work in childcare because they love children and appreciate being part of something bigger than themselves. In most cases they could make more money doing something else. Your job is to help them do their best work. It's also to help people grow and develop so they become better at what they do.

Do what top performing supervisors do. They show up a lot! Your team will get used to you being around. Have conversations with your team. I mean real conversations between adults, where both of you talk and listen. The conversations should be about work issues, but also about other things like soccer games, children, or hobbies. Those conversations help you form relationships that make many things you must do easier and more likely to succeed. Your team should become better by being associated with you.

Top-performing supervisors care for their people. So help your staff, parents, and children deal with the stress of life today. Watch for signs of high stress and burnout. Develop a list of local resources that can offer help. Be flexible and compassionate.

Take care of yourself. Get enough sleep, eat sensibly, and exercise. Give yourself time off to restore energy and balance. You can't pour from an empty cup. An excellent book on taking care of yourself is Tom Rath's *Eat, Move, Sleep.*

One More Thing—Be Prepared

As my time in the Scouting program taught me, Be Prepared. Never has a statement been more relevant than owning or operating a childcare center. When you spend your day with lots of children, you must be prepared for surprises. Alissa Thompson of New Beginnings Preschool had one of the most amazing incidents I've heard of. In her own words:

> *I had a teacher in the one-year-old room who was working by herself, and we had a bad classroom door. While she was changing one child, the other kids were working on the door together, pushing it open. They got it open, but it was heavy, and so it came back, and it severed somebody's finger, and we had to find the finger in the door jamb, throw it on ice, and run it down to the children's hospital so they could sew it back on.*

You may not ever have a situation like that one, but I guarantee you that you will have lots of situations where you must keep your wits about you. Here's Heather Torres again from Hope Lutheran Learning Center:

> *One time, I actually had a set of grandparents show up to pick up their grandson. They weren't on the pickup list.*
>
> *And the little boy saw them, said, "Hi, Grandma." And she's like, "Oh, that's okay." And I said, "Well no, we can't release him to you because you're not on the list." Grandma actually called the police on me. I couldn't get ahold of Mom and Dad, and she couldn't get ahold of Mom and Dad.*
>
> *And so the police actually showed up, and she said, "They're refusing to release my grandson to me." So, of course, I sound like a terrible person. But then I said to the police officers, "Well, they're not on the pickup list. I don't know if they actually are Grandma and Grandpa, and a child calling them Grandma is not identification enough." And the police were like, "You know what? You're right." And so we had to wait there for Mom and Dad, and it was super awkward.*

You and your staff should know your policies and procedures and follow them. But you can be sure that there will be things where you must be flexible and think on your feet. It's part of the business.

So far, we've discussed how to hire the right people and how to manage your operations. Now it's time for the final chapter in the book. It's about your building.

Your Building

I ***love working with childcare owners*** and operators. I've learned I can make an important contribution to a childcare operation because a physical location is central to the childcare organization's mission and success.

In an earlier chapter, we talked about finding the right location for your childcare center. When you're in the right location, the families and communities you want to serve can find you easily. This chapter is about completing that loop. It's about creating a facility where you can profitably achieve your childcare objectives. More than that, it's a place where you will be spending a lot of time, so you should create a pleasant place for you to work; a place that brings you joy.

Your building is where that all comes together. In this chapter, you'll learn how to assemble a team of experts to help you create a building where you can serve clients effectively and profitably. You'll learn why the look and feel of your center is important and how to create a facility where you can meet all the national, state, and local regulations. Let's start with the people who will help make your center a reality.

Assemble a Building Team

"None of us knows as much as all of us." I don't know who first said that, but it's certainly true in childcare. That's why you need a team of experts. The physical location where you do childcare must meet many different requirements.

Your childcare center must meet national, state, and local regulations governing childcare. Your building must meet zoning and building code requirements. Building codes and licensing requirements are two different things. Different government bodies created them to meet different needs. With all that, you need to be able to run a profitable operation.

The effective childcare building teams I've seen include four kinds of experts. There should be a commercial real estate broker, an architect, a contractor, and the licensing surveyor. Your experts should meet two requirements.

They should have childcare experience. Childcare facilities must meet licensing requirements. They should be designed to help you meet your operational and profitability goals. Mine your own network for expert recommendations on who can help you accomplish the requirements you have for your building. When you've engaged one expert, ask him or her for recommendations for the other experts.

Your experts should be the kind of people who put the children's interests first. When I interviewed architects and contractors for this book, I was amazed how often they came back to the needs of the children. As Joe Perkins, a well-known and respected childcare contractor, put it:

These are kids. Your kids, my kids, and other kids that will be in this center. And what's the most important thing we want for our kids when we're dropping them off in the morning? It's safety and security, right?

Licensing requirements are there to keep the children safe. An effective team won't ignore the specifics of those requirements. Instead, they'll find creative ways to meet them and make an effective childcare center.

Effective, in that last sentence, means well-run and profitable. Without profit, you can't continue in business. Without profit, you can't pay your teachers what they deserve, and you won't be able to attract and keep great teachers. Without profit, you don't have money for maintenance. The bottom line is, without profit, you can't have a good childcare center; in fact, there won't be a center at all. So, design must account for all the regulations and the profitability of the center.

The experts you hire are important, but don't let them overwhelm you. Ask for clarification about things you don't understand. Ask for honest feedback from your experts when making design decisions. Your team members will have expertise you don't have, but you're the one who ultimately must make and be responsible for design choices. Be confident throughout this process; there's no such thing as a dumb question.

Functionality: How Does Your Building Work as a Childcare Center?

Your mission determines the kind of building you need. You created an avatar and specified the services you will offer in the chapter on the marketing plan. Childcare center expert architect Ken Eller shared the following examples with me.

Some centers offer what amounts to organized babysitting. They keep the children clean and safe, but they don't do much more than that. In some cases, that's fine because that's what some families want.

Other childcare centers have a mission of preparing children for school. Those childcare operators want to provide some instruction so children will end up school-ready. They believe that a solid grounding before school will help children get the most from whatever school they attend. These centers will be more elaborately designed.

There are also centers that want to go beyond just preparing children for school. They want to prepare them for lifetime learning. Montessori is an example. A center with a goal like that will need more multipurpose, open space.

It seems like this should be simple, but it usually isn't. For example, if your mission is to help children become school-ready, you may consider buying an old school building as a facility. That seems like it should work, but it often doesn't. You'll need to make many changes to the building to meet licensing requirements.

When you're making changes to your building, you may be tempted to cut corners. Cutting corners isn't a good idea if you're also overlooking licensing requirements. Ken Eller is very specific about the right thing to do.

> *I have very little tolerance for any kind of compromise. I make it very clear to my clients that there are*

rules and regulations, and they're there for all of their safety. They're not to be toyed with. I won't tolerate that. I won't allow it. I won't be party to anything that would compromise anything.

If you're clear about what your goal is as a childcare operator, you can decide the kind of facility you need. This is a judgement of value and a determination about how you can provide the most value to the families that entrust their children to you. There will always be tradeoffs. The people on your building team can help you understand the tradeoffs that are possible and help you make informed decisions.

Design: How Does Your Building Look and Feel?

This should be a relatively simple exercise for you. Imagine for a moment that you're a childcare teacher. What kind of place would you like to work in? Now imagine you're a parent considering various childcare centers for your child. Imagine where you would like your child to spend the majority of their time. Just as adults should be mindful of where they work and who they work with, parents need to be mindful of where their children are and who they spend their time with.

What would you look for? What would impress you? What would turn you off?

The design of your center sends a message. It sends a message to prospective teachers that your center would be a good place to work. It sends a message to parents about the quality of childcare and the services you offer.

Appearance is important. Yes, you must meet all licensing requirements, but parents will judge you on whether your center looks like a place they want to send their child.

There's more to think about too. What about smells? For human beings, smells are a powerful sense. If a parent walks in your door and smells a foul odor of some kind, he or she may decide, right there, that your center is not a place for their child. An experienced childcare building team can make a difference. An inexperienced team will follow the licensing requirements and put in the exhaust fans that are required. But experienced childcare architects will go a step farther. Architect Ken Eller, for example, will put small exhaust fans over diaper changing stations, too.

Maintenance is important. You want to maintain your center in the best possible condition so it makes a positive impression on parents and, more importantly, ensures the safety of the children. Regular maintenance also helps you keep up with licensing requirements.

Some maintenance activities are routine tasks that are part of your task list. They include things like picking up things from the floor, wiping high touch surfaces, and empyting wastebaskets.

You should also pay attention to the maintenance of your center. It's a good idea to have a regular service agreement with a contractor or a property manager who can spot things that should be fixed and fix them. I suggest that you use two documents to stay on top of regular maintenance.

A basic checklist for what needs to be done on a day-to-day basis. In addition, a log of repairs can be a place where you enter things that you know need to be fixed. You can show those to your maintenance contractor and have them sign off when the repair is done. Keep the log in your maintenance folder so you can show it when you have a licensing inspection.

Licensing

Childcare licensing and regulations are there to protect the children. Keeping up with evolving licensing requirements and keeping your facility up to a high standard should be part of the way you operate.

Get to know your licensing surveyor. Cordial professional relationships help you get more done, when it comes to meeting licensing requirements. You don't have to like your licensing surveyor. But you'll do better if you get along with him or her.

As we've discussed, Childcare has its own licensing requirements you need to meet. They're not the same as building codes. Your challenge is to accomplish your childcare mission, meet both civil codes and licensing requirements, and make a profit. Lean on the knowledge and experience of your team. There are always tradeoffs in the ways you can meet licensing requirements and your business objectives.

Your building is where everything comes together. This is where you keep the promises you make in your marketing. Your building is where the care in childcare happens.

Conclusion

We've ***covered a lot of ground*** in this book. I hope I've given you tools and resources to make your childcare center successful and an influence for good in your community. Truly successful centers elevate and inspire everyone around them.

Other childcare books focus on working *in* your business but this book attempts to focus on working *on* your business. *No matter how good your program is, without good business management, you won't be a successful childcare center for long.*

Children Come First

Children should come first in curriculum and teaching decisions. They should come first in maintenance and security decisions. And children should come first in every business decision.

I quoted Ted Batycki on this in the Introduction. It's worth quoting him again.

> *What's right for children is right for our business. We ask ourselves that question all the time. And so, we talk about our business. We understand the finances, we understand how to make money in this business. But we always ask ourselves, "Are we doing this because it's right for the children, or are we doing it because it's right for the business?" And if it's only because it's right for the business, that's not a good reason to do it.*

Every decision you make and every action you take should be tested with Ted's question: "Are we doing this because it's right for the children?"

Make Your Business as Good as Your Childcare

Good business practices assure that your business runs smoothly and lets your staff give full attention to the children. Good business practices make it possible for you to stay in business for a long time. Here are some things to pay attention to.

Your accounting system should make sure that bills get paid on time. Use your budget to stay on top of where you are financially. Work with a professional advisor to make sure you balance your budget and pay your taxes on time.

Develop a simple marketing plan. Enroll. Enroll. Enroll. This is a key to success. You don't have a business if you don't have children in your center. Become a marketing machine.

Use checklists and effective systems and processes to stay on top of maintenance, licensing, and other issues. Make sure that routine tasks are done routinely.

Do your due diligence whenever you're facing a major decision. Big decisions like whether to expand, where to locate, or how to remodel your facility have long-term consequences. Give them the research and discussion they deserve.

Don't try to go it alone. Surround yourself with good people. Use all the brains you can get to help you. Talk to other childcare operators. Engage experts to help you.

It's All About the "WHO"

People and relationships are the most important things in business and in life. Cultivate good working relationships with everyone around you.

Your teachers and staff are the people who live out your mission and your core values. Give them fair compensation and a good place to work. Help them develop their skills and to become who they want to become.

Your children and their parents decide whether to attend your center or go somewhere else. They're also your word-of-mouth marketing. Treat them like the valued partners they are. Help them understand what you do and how they can help you do it better.

Lenders and surveyors are people you may not see all that often. Don't forget them when they are out of sight. Thank them for their help. Keep them informed about what you're doing. Stay in touch.

Help your team of experts serve you well. Engage the best experts you can. Then, engage *with* them so you understand their advice. Keep them up to date on what and how you're doing.

Always Be Improving

The world won't stand still, so you must keep getting better. If you're not growing, you're dying.

Success leaves clues. Look around you at other successful childcare centers in your area. Read about other centers' success. Go to conferences. Talk with other childcare operators. Engage consultants and professionals who have seen what works from a 30,000-foot view.

Don't be afraid to try new things. The childcare industry needs to continue to improve and adapt in how to best care for children in our constantly evolving world. The quickest way to find out if an idea will work for you, or how you should change it to make it work for you, is to try it. To quote Yoda from *Star Wars*: "Do or do not, there is no try."

Develop habits of success. Successful people in all walks of life tend to develop habits that help them to be successful. Block out time for important work. Then, hold it sacred. Do important things first. Spend a little time every day working on your business to make it better.

Childcare is noble work. The work you do touches children and their families. The impact of your work stretches into the future. The children you care for and educate will shape a future that you may not see. That's why you put children at the center of your concerns and your choices.

Doing the work of childcare well demands that you make your business practices as good as your childcare. Then you have the facilities and resources to do excellent childcare. When you make good business practice routine, you free your time to concentrate on childcare.

I shared the advice and insights of successful childcare operators in these pages. I hope you will draw knowledge, strength, and inspiration from them. I hope this book will help you and your childcare center succeed.

This is the end of the book, but it's just the beginning of your childcare adventure. Check out the information in the Appendices. Visit the book web page. I'd love to hear from you about what you've learned. Please contact me if I can help you in any way. I'd love to help you and your childcare center succeed.

Appendices

Formal Business Plans for Loan and Grant Applications

The chapter on effective planning discussed why planning is important and introduced you to the planning sweet spot. We also looked at marketing plans and budgets as simplified business plans. Each got their own chapter. So why do we need this Appendix about formal business plans?

Every childcare center can use those simplified plans to guide choices every day. They're for internal use.

The time may come when you need to borrow money. It may be when you're just starting your center and need a loan for start-up costs and working capital. It may be when you need a cash infusion to survive a disaster like an earthquake, fire, or pandemic. Or it may be when you want or need cash to acquire a commercial property.

When that time comes, potential lenders will expect you to go through a formal evaluation process. They will require a formal business plan that demonstrates your need for funds and your plan to pay back the loan. There will probably be several parts to the application, but the formal business plan is a key way to demonstrate that you know your business.

As I mentioned, early in my career I helped create outlines for small businesses to use for their formal business plans. There are many books and articles written specifically on business plans. This Appendix is a general overview.

The plan will outline your strategy and financial projections for your childcare center. You'll want to be as thorough in your financial projections as possible. You will prepare *pro forma* statements based on your projections. Recall that *pro formas* are statements that you use to share your expected financial results. They may be the most important part of your loan request.

As I mentioned in the introduction, Ted Batycki was a commercial banker where he spent his time reviewing loan applications before he and his wife started Natural Choice Academy in Phoenix. Ted told me about the loan application process:

> *At the end of the day, most banks are not going to read the narrative of your business plan with a lot of passion. They're going to read the projections. I can tell you right now, when I was a banker, and I was not the only one that did this; we would get twenty-thirty-forty-page business plans, and we would go straight to the exhibits because that's where the pro formas are.*

An experienced childcare teacher can walk into a classroom and tell very quickly if the teacher there knows what he or she is doing. When an experienced lender looks at your *pro formas*, he or she will immediately know the answer to an important question. Ted phrases the question this way: "Does this person know their stuff?"

The people who will decide whether to loan you money probably don't know a lot about childcare. They're financial people, and it's natural for them to judge you primarily based on financial criteria.

There are many accountants and financial advisors who can assist with the financial component of your business. Reach out to other childcare owners to find vendors who know the industry and are proven to be trustworthy. Read the relevant chapters in this book for guidance on some areas of the plan.

A Formal Business Plan Outline

Here is a general outline for developing your business plan. Your lender may have their own preferred form. I prepared this outline for people setting up a new child-care center.

Remember that the purpose of your plan is to demonstrate to a potential lender that you know your stuff.

Title Page

This should include your center name, your name (and your partners' names if you have any), contact information, the date, and the name of the organization or investor you are submitting the business plan to for consideration.

Table of Contents

This should include section titles and page numbers to identify their location in the plan. Be sure to include any added sections to your plan in the Table of Contents.

Example Outline

- Executive Summary
- Industry Description
- Market Analysis
- Program Summary
- Operations
- Marketing
- Management and Staffing
- Strategic Planning
- Financial Operations and Projections

Executive Summary

The executive summary should be a short summary of the key points in your business plan.

Industry Description

Provide a brief description of the childcare industry.

Market Analysis

Describe the local market for childcare. You'll want to profile the childcare centers in your area and identify opportunities. Use maps or charts to show nearby centers (highlight size and population). Feature how your center will stand out. Use graphs or charts to show demographics in the area.

Program Summary

Describe your program/curriculum in detail. Include a description of the families and children you serve and how they benefit from your programs.

Operations

Describe the day-to-day operation of your center. Include descriptions of your procedures for meeting licensing requirements, maintaining the facility, and dealing with emergencies.

Marketing

Describe your marketing plan. Cover advertising and marketing activities. Be sure to mention your plans for community involvement, generating word of mouth, and courting parent referrals.

Management and Staffing

Include short bios of people in management. Also include information on why they're qualified for the positions they hold.

Describe what professional roles you must fill. Outline your strategy for finding and hiring the right people for all your roles.

Include the names and brief descriptions of board members.

Strategic Planning

Describe how you will open your center and set up your systems and processes for running the business. Here are some things you may want to consider.

- Timeline for opening your center
- Include the center's startup budget and source of funds
- Initial and staggered enrollment figures accompanied by expenses and revenue
- Budget projections and a timeline for the center to become profitable
- Specific requests for funds and repay time frame

Be sure to give a realistic and obtainable goal that will show your capability of opening and operating a childcare center. But, make sure you ask for enough money to do what you want. Here's the experience of two childcare owners.

Alissa Thompson

I got an SBA loan, and that was the route that I took. And I think I lowballed way too much. And so, that's where stress came into play. I only got an $85,000 loan, and I really should have gotten an $185,000 loan. But I didn't want to get myself in a position where I had to pay back a bunch of money. So, for me, I think the biggest struggle was the first year, not having enough capital.

Ted Batycki

I am a pretty good financial analyst, and I still missed the mark. People ask me, "What was the biggest mistake you made starting your business?" The biggest one was we underestimated just how much startup capital is really necessary. When we went to the bank and borrowed money, we should have borrowed a lot more.

Financial Operations and Projections

This is the place for your financial projections, budget, and *pro formas*. Include the assumptions you used to develop your projections. This is an important section for you to demonstrate you know your stuff.

Throughout this book, I've stressed the importance of working with a team of experts. Keep that in mind when it's time to draft a formal business plan.

Cost of Care

(Example)

RONALD V. MCGUCKIN AND ASSOCIATES
Post Office Box 2126
Bristol, Pennsylvania 19007
215-785-3400 215-785-3401 (FAX)
Childproviderlaw.com (website)

ACTUAL COST OF CARE AND BREAK-EVEN ANALYSIS

The Children's Center
Operating Budget vs. Actual Dollars Spent

INCOME	ACTUAL	BUDGET
Tuition	270,400	312,000
Foundation Grants	0	2,500
Individual Contributions	550	1,250
TOTAL INCOME	**270,950**	**315,750**

EXPENSES	ACTUAL FIXED	ACTUAL VAR.	ACTUAL TOTAL	BUDGET
Director	21,000	0	21,000	21,000
Asst. Director	16,000	0	16,000	13,000
Teaching Staff	10,000	125,000	135,000	150,000
Taxes and Ins.	2,000	13,000	15,000	12,000
Staff Development	0	250	250	2,000
Program Activities	0	2,000	2,000	2,000
Supplies and Materials	0	7,000	7,000	10,000
Food	0	16,000	16,000	16,000
Building Rent	28,000	2,000	30,000	30,000
Utilities	2,000	4,200	6,200	5,000
Janitorial	2,000	8,000	10,000	8,000
Taxes and Ins.	4,500	0	4,500	4,500
Depreciation	7,300	0	7,300	7,300
Van Rental/Mileage	750	2,500	3,250	2,000
Gas	0	850	850	750
Insurance	1,200	0	1,200	1,200
Accounting/Legal Fees	3,000	5,000	8,000	3,000
Supplies	0	2,400	2,400	3,000
Telephone	750	1,450	2,200	2,500
Insurance	1,000	10,500	11,500	12,000
Dues/Subscriptions	0	500	500	500
Licenses	0	1,000	1,000	1,000
Travel/Entertainment	0	600	600	1,000
Bad Debt Expense	0	3,750	3,750	2,000
Advertising	0	500	500	500
Misc.	0	4,000	4,000	3,500
Profit Projection				2,000
TOTAL EXPENSES	**99,500**	**210,500**	**310,000**	**315,750**

ENROLLMENT DATA
The Children's Center

Full-Time Tuition	$80/week	$16/day
Licensed Capacity	100	
Revenue Capacity	$416,000	
Actual Tuition Revenue	$270,400	

Tuition is charged for 52 weeks/year. The center is open 262 days per year.

Cost of Care Analysis: How much does is cost this center to provide services to one child for one day?

Total Expenses / number of children / number of days open = Total Cost/child/day

$310,000.00 / 65 children / 262 days = $18.23

Enrollment

	Capacity	**Current**
Young Toddlers	10	8
Older Toddlers	10	6
Preschool (3's)	40	25
Preschool (4's)	40	26
Total Enrollment	**100**	**65**

How many children would this center need to enroll to Break-even at the current tuition rate?

Calculating the Break-Even Point

First, Calculate the Variable Cost Percentage:

Variable Cost / Tuition (or Revenue) = Variable Cost Percentage

Second, Calculate the Break-Even Dollar Amount

Fixed Cost / 1 – Variable Cost Percentage = Break-Even Point in Dollars

Third, Calculate the Break-Even Enrollment

Break-Even Dollar Amount / Operating weeks / Weekly Tuition = # of Children needed to Break-Even

Does this agency even have the ability to Break-even at the current tuition rate charged?

What are some suggestions for improving the financial status of this agency? (Short Term vs. Long Term)

Calculate the Break-even Point if tuition was raised to a subsidy reimbursement rate of $24.80/day ($124/wk).

Reading List

"The more that you read, the more things you will know. The more that you learn, the more places you'll go."

—Dr. Seuss

I ***'m an avid reader***, and I've learned that all kinds of books inspire me. Only one book on this list is specifically about childcare. All of them have had a positive influence on me personally or professionally, and I believe each could help you better succeed in business and in life. They are presented in no particular order.

Business Books

The Ultimate Child Care Marketing Guide: Tactics, Tools, and Strategies for Success by Kris Murray

The E Myth: Why Most Businesses Don't Work and What to Do About It by Michael Gerber

Good to Great: Why Some Companies Make the Leap . . . And Others Don't by Jim Collins

How to Win Friends & Influence People by Dale Carnegie

Start with Why: How Great Leaders Inspire Everyone to Take Action by Simon Sinek

Grit: The Power of Passion and Perseverance by Angela Duckworth

Atomic Habits: An Easy & Proven Way to Build Good Habits & Break Bad Ones by James Clear

How Will You Measure Your Life? by Clayton M. Christensen, James Allworth, and Karen Dillon

Standing for Something: 10 Neglected Virtues That Will Heal Our Hearts and Homes by Gordon B. Hinckley

Getting More: How You Can Negotiate to Succeed in Work and Life by Stuart Diamond

Think and Grow Rich by Napoleon Hill

Getting Things Done: The Art of Stress-Free Productivity by David Allen

The 5 Languages of Appreciation in the Workplace: Empowering Organizations by Encouraging People by Gary Chapman and Paul White

Mindset: The New Psychology of Success by Carol S. Dweck

Who Not How: The Formula to Achieve Bigger Goals Through Accelerating Teamwork by Dan Sullivan and Benjamin Hardy

Eat, Move, Sleep: How Small Choices Lead to Big Changes by Tom Rath

Children's Books

Oh, the Places You'll Go! Deluxe Edition by Dr. Seuss

What Do You Do with an Idea? by Kobi Yamada and Mae Besom

The Giving Tree by Shel Silverstein

The Complete Tales of Winnie-the-Pooh by A. A. Milne

You're Here for a Reason by Nancy Tillman

Love You Forever by Robert Munsch and Sheila McGraw

The Complete Adventures of Curious George: 75th Anniversary Edition by H. A. Rey and Margret Rey

Pajama Time! by Sandra Boynton

You Are Special by Max Lucado

Acknowledgments

W***riting this book*** was one of the hardest things I've ever done. I have experienced every feeling of self-doubt and self-consciousness one can experience; I regularly thought to myself, "I have no business writing a book." Through it all, I am happy to present this work to my past, present, and future self as a testament that I can do hard things and to all my wonderful friends and colleagues in the early childhood industry, as I'm confident it will be a great resource to you.

I am grateful to my Father in Heaven and my Savior every day for how truly blessed I am. I am so grateful to know that God is in the details of our lives.

Laurisa, you are the love and joy of my life! I thank Heavenly Father every day for the life we share together. I am so blessed! Thank you for your unwavering love and support in all that I do.

To my four beautiful children, thank you for loving me unconditionally and for the daily reminders that the most important work I will ever do is within the walls of my own home. I am so blessed to be your dad.

I'm fortunate to be in business with my brothers Tanner and Stuart.

Tanner, you're who I've always wanted to be when I grow up. Thank you for your example and your friendship. You taught me how to work and that if you're not growing, you're dying! Your thirst for knowledge is contagious, and this book is a byproduct of your example over all these years.

Stuart, thank you for your positivity and unwavering support. Your joyful outlook on life and overall goodness is a joy to be around. Your daily example reminds me to keep my priorities in check.

To my parents, thank you for your patience and for always being my biggest fans! From the countless trips to the principal's office on my behalf to the endless sports practices and games, thank you for loving me and supporting me. I've never once had to question your love, and now as a parent, I try to follow your loving examples every day.

To my sister Julie and all my other family, thank you for your unconditional love and support.

I want to thank my entire team at Menlo Group for your friendship and support. You truly are my home away from home, and I am so blessed to have you in my life. You make me better in all aspects of my life, each and every day.

None of this would have been possible without my writing coach and friend, Wally Bock. You helped turn my scrambled thoughts and ideas into something I could be proud of. You are a master of your craft, and I am truly grateful that you agreed to share your talents with me. I am honored to call you my friend!

A huge shout-out to Blaine Strickland for helping me to come up with a game plan in the early stages. Your friendship and advice are truly appreciated.

This book wouldn't have been possible without the countless individual providers, companies, and organizations that have allowed me to assist them in one form or another. Thank you for allowing me to be a part of your childcare journey.

I owe an enormous debt of gratitude to those who were influential in making this book a reality, including, in alphabetical order: Ted Batycki, Lori Buxton, Diana Darmawaskita, Sean Diana, Ron Duhart, Andrea Dunlop, Ken Eller, Kensey Gabbard, Robert Haggard, Elana Hillel, Brooke Loeffler, Kelly McCready, Ron McGuckin, Nicole Newhouse, Joe and Katie Perkins, Martha Picciao, Barbie Prinster, Raegina Rico, Tonya Sevilla, Keith Slater, Alissa Thompson, and Heather Torres. You freely gave of your time and talents to assist in putting this book together.

Thank you for having such a positive influence on my life. I am truly grateful to know you.

Many of the ideas in this book are not new. I am truly grateful for tremendous business leaders and visionaries, inside and outside the childcare industry, who continue to share their ideas with the world.

A big thank-you to all my friends and anyone who has been an influence for good in my life. I am a better person for having known you.

A big thank-you also to anyone who reads this book. Thank you for your time and thank you for the good you have done AND will do in the childcare industry! Our children are counting on you.

—Grafton

About the Author

G*rafton Milne* has worked with many different child-care owners and directors throughout the child-care industry. In writing this book, he had the pleasure of working with childcare experts across the country to learn Childcare Center Success. As a result, he provides a unique perspective from a 30,000-foot view of what it takes to run a successful childcare center. Grafton has earned his Certified Commercial Investment Member (CCIM) and Society of Industrial and Office Realtors (SIOR) designations, signifying that globally, he is among those at the top of his field in commercial real estate. With a one-of-a-kind niche in childcare real estate, Grafton is affiliated and involved in many national and local early childhood organizations. He's an Ironman Triathlete and enjoys scuba diving and anything else that lets him experience the world with the people he loves. Grafton lives in Phoenix, Arizona, with his wife, Laurisa and their four amazing children.

You can reach Grafton via this book's web page.

grafton@menlocre.com

www.ingramcontent.com/pod-product-compliance
Lightning Source LLC
LaVergne TN
LVHW050846160826
845684LV00012B/72/J

9798985438109